SURVIVING BIEN HOA

Steve Crews

Order this book online at www.trafford.com
or email orders@trafford.com

Most Trafford titles are also available at major online book
retailers.

Cover design, book design, all photos
by Steve Crews

Printed in the United States of America.

ISBN: 978-1-4669-4305-6 (sc)
ISBN: 978-1-4669-4306-3 (hc)
ISBN: 978-1-4669-4307-0 (e)

Library of Congress Control Number: 2012910696

Trafford rev. 06/11/2012

 www.trafford.com

North America & international
toll-free: 1 888 232 4444 (USA & Canada)
phone: 250 383 6864 ♦ fax: 812 355 4082

I visited the Vietnam Veterans Memorial
in Washington, D.C. on Memorial Day May 31,
1999. Seeing those 58,219 names just blew
me away. I cried for all of them, their
families and this country. Who knows what
great things they might have accomplished
had they lived.

I noticed that some people had left some
mementos at the base of the memorial and I
did as well. I had written a poem a few
years before that was inspired by a painting
I'd seen and I gave it the title of "The
Wall." It was copyrighted and published in
1996. This book and that poem are dedicated
to those 58,219 people whose names are on
the Vietnam Veterans Memorial.

THE WALL

The names appeared before me
Out of the gray Washington mist
Each one of them a person once
Added to the Grim Reaper's list

I wondered why they all had died
So far away from their homes
Some arrived in one piece, perhaps
Others returned only as bones

It's sad to see some people here
They find a name, then cry
And wonder often, for all to hear
Why was it <u>they</u> didn't die

They say our best died in Vietnam
I'm not sure who to blame
But I've seen some here at this wall
Veterans, searching for a name

The wall, the names, and the visitors
All faded in the dreary gray
As I turned and wiped away a tear
And saluted THE WALL that day

INTRODUCTION

When I was in junior high in Oklahoma back in the early 1960s, I read a book, Guadalcanal Diary. It was about one man's World War II experiences during the battle for Guadalcanal in 1942. Even though I didn't keep a diary when I was in Vietnam, that book I'd read inspired me to write a book about my own wartime experiences. I figured that if one guy could do it, then so could I.

Inspiration is one thing, doing it is another. I needed a reason for doing it that went beyond just inspiration. I thought that if I didn't write this book, nobody would ever know what it was like for me and the untold experiences would be taken to my grave. No one would ever know how I got on a plane as a boy and a year later got on another plane as a man and the changes that took place in my life during that year.

While my story isn't as exciting as others I've read about that dealt with the same war, many others who served in Vietnam will be able to relate to the places I went to, the sights, smells, cultural differences and dangers of just being in Vietnam at any given time. Some Vietnam veterans will agree with me when I say that, there were times in Vietnam when, if you had not seen things with your own eyes, you'd have doubted things happened the way they did. Everything in this book is true and needed to be told. It's that simple.

PREFACE

The war in Vietnam seemed to drag on
forever. The first time I ever heard of the
place was in the 5th grade. One of my classmates at Steed Elementary School in Midwest
City, Oklahoma told me that his father was
there. That was in 1961.

During the 1960s, war movies like The
Longest Day and TV shows like Combat were my
favorites to watch as I saw Americans in
combat winning battles large and small.
World War II for us lasted from December
1941 to September 1945.

When I enlisted in the Air Force in
1971, the war in Vietnam was still going on
after ten long years. With the help of our
allies, we'd defeated Japan, Germany and
Italy, fighting all over the world in only
four years. In World War II the nation was
united. GIs returning home from the war were
given parades. In 1971 the nation was divided. Some GIs returning home from Vietnam
were spat upon and called "baby killers" by
some of their fellow citizens. The streets
were often filled with marchers protesting
the war. There were no "welcome home" parades in most cities.

President Nixon had begun a "Vietnamization" process to get our troops out of
Vietnam. We were training the South Vietnamese how to conduct the war by themselves
and use the planes, tanks, helicopters and
other military weapons we supplied them with
to carry on the war without us. The American
presence in Vietnam had been reduced from
over 500,000 in 1968 to about 150,000 at the
beginning of 1971.

With little popular support back home
and a no-win situation in Vietnam, GIs in
Vietnam faced the prospect of dying for a

lost cause. Morale within the American military units suffered. One of my tech school
instructors had been stationed at Tuy Hoa
Air Base in Vietnam. He told the class one
day, "You may not smoke or drink or cuss
right now, but after a year in Vietnam you
will!" He was right.

The nightly news on TV and the newspapers continually showed the anti-war pro-
tests including people burning their draft
cards. They dwelled on bad situations within the military like the My Lai massacre and
the drug problem that was getting really bad.
The drug toll for American soldiers was so
bad by the end of 1971 that approximately
20,500 required treatment for serious drug
abuse while less than 5,000 soldiers were
treated in hospitals for combat wounds. The
favorite slogan that was chanted by anti-war
protesters was "Hell no, we won't go" and
some of them even moved to Canada to avoid
being drafted into the U.S. armed forces.
Years later, another U.S. president granted
those who fled their own country amnesty.

Then there were a few of us who voluntarily enlisted in the military, some even
dropping out of college to do so. Some did
out of a sense of patriotism, or felt it
was their civic duty. Some people enlisted
so they would be able to choose which branch
of the military they would serve in instead
of waiting and having someone else choose
for them. No matter how they got to Vietnam
or why, it was a messed up war they had to
contend with. Welcome to my world!

American Air Force personnel had been
stationed at Bien Hoa Air Base as early as
1961. The Air Force trained Vietnamese
pilots how to fly the North American T-28
Trojan, which our own pilots used strictly
as a training plane. The Vietnamese Air
Force (VNAF) used the single engine, propeller-driven trainer as a fighter/bomber

by mounting small bombs and rocket launchers under the wings. Most of the time American pilots sat in the back seat of the two-seater plane as advisers.

The first T-28s to arrive at Bien Hoa Air Base came from Hurlburt Field, Florida and belonged to Detachment A, 4400th Combat Crew Training Squadron. These planes were a part of Operation Farmgate and carried VNAF markings.

By 1964, Bien Hoa Air Base played an even larger role in the war in Vietnam. The U.S. Air Force had B-57 Canberra twin-engine jet bombers stationed there by then. Bien Hoa made headline news when, on the night of October 31, 1964 the Viet Cong staged a mortar attack on the base. Four U.S. military personnel were killed and several were wounded. Twenty seven aircraft, including some B-57s were damaged and destroyed.

Bien Hoa Air Base also had some Fairchild C-123 Providers, twin engine propeller driven cargo planes that were used from January 1965 to February 1971 in a defoliation program called Operation Ranch Hand. These aircraft sprayed Agent Orange, a toxic chemical herbicide to kill vegetation and give the enemy less cover to hide in. The defoliant caused long-lasting health problems to thousands of Vietnamese and Americans who came into contact with it. These planes from Bien Hoa also sprayed a defoliant called Agent Blue. It was made of 100% sodium cacodylic acid which is an arsenic compound. Although the organic compound was not as toxic as the inorganic forms of arsenic, such as sodium arsenite, it can be fatal to humans. Agent Blue was also used from 1965 to 1971. That added another element of danger to being stationed at Bien Hoa Air Base.

Bell aircraft company designed the AH-1G Huey Cobra attack helicopter for the

U.S. Army. In August 1967, the first operational Cobras in Vietnam were flown by the 334th Armed Helicopter Company stationed at Bien Hoa Air Base. It was the fastest and most heavily armed helicopter used in the war.

During the Tet Offensive of 1968, Bien Hoa Air Base was attacked by enemy ground troops, mortars and rockets. The Huey Cobras stationed there helped save the base from being overrun. Over a hundred dead enemy soldiers were killed while trying to get through the barbed wire perimeter on the U.S. side of the base.

And now, ten years after the first Air Force personnel were stationed here and ten years after I'd first heard of Vietnam, I was there. I didn't know much about the place at first, but in time I would. So many others had survived their tours of duty there and I figured that surviving Bien Hoa was something that I could do too.

CHAPTER ONE

OCTOBER 1971

As the month of October began, I was at
home in rural Coweta County, Georgia on
leave. I lived near the town of Sharpsburg
at the time. I'd already completed Air
Force basic training and the Air Passenger
Service tech school and was given the opportunity to take a 30-day leave. At the time,
everyone in my tech school who got orders to
Vietnam could do that and my class of twelve
did, except for one guy who failed the last
test and was set back in training and ended
up with a different assignment.

Everyone living east of the Mississippi
River would fly to Vietnam from McGuire Air
Force Base, New Jersey on October 23, 1971.
Everyone living west of that river would fly
from Travis Air Force Base, California on
October 28, 1971.

When my leave was over, I said goodbye
to my two younger brothers at home before
they went to school. I was the oldest of
three boys. I had no sisters. Then my
parents drove me to the airport in Atlanta.
My mother started crying during our final
goodbye and last hugs. That almost got me
choked up as I boarded the plane bound for
Philadelphia.

As I sat on the plane and tried to get a
last look at my parents through the window,
I couldn't help but wonder if I'd made the
right decision. I didn't have to go to
Vietnam. I'd been given a choice. During
the out-processing appointments I went to at
Sheppard Air Force Base, at one briefing we
were all told that anyone who was a sole-
surviving son could opt-out of their Vietnam
assignment just by signing a form they had.
They gave us the definition of a sole-surviving son and I fit that definition. My

biological father died in Korea during the
Korean War six days before my first birthday.
I was his only child. My brothers were born
after my mother remarried. Therefore, by
law, I didn't have to go to Vietnam. If I
died there, that would be the end of my part
of the family tree. When the briefer said to
raise your hand if you were a sole-surviving
son, I kept my hand down.

My step-father had been in the Korean War
too and his brother-in-law had been to Vietnam twice while assigned to the Army Special
Forces (Green Berets) and I didn't want someone to think I was a coward or that I chick-
ened out. I may be stupid, I thought, but
I'm no coward.

Unsure at that time if I had made the
right decision, later I felt that I had. The
experience of serving in Vietnam helped me to
better understand the meaning of the words on
the lighter given to me by my commanding officer just before I left Bien Hoa: "One has
not lived 'til he has almost died. Life has
a flavor the protected will never know." How
true!

I got off the plane in Philadelphia and
called my grandparents from a pay phone in the
terminal. My mother's parents lived in Toms
River, New Jersey then. I spent the night
with them and they drove me to McGuire Air
Force Base the next day.

We said our goodbyes and then I checked in
for my flight. I saw some of my tech school
classmates in the terminal. We were separated
during the boarding of the plane due to the
seat assignments we got. We all ended up sitting next to total strangers, most of them
from different branches of the service. All
of the passengers I saw were wearing military
uniforms, most of them in the Army. The only
females I saw were the stewardesses.

I noticed that one of my classmates who
lived east of the Mississippi River didn't get

on the plane. I later found out from a
friend who got a letter from him a couple of
weeks later that he missed a small commuter
plane connecting flight while traveling from
his home to Philadelphia. Since it wasn't
his fault, he didn't get into any trouble.
Once he got to McGuire Air Force Base and our
plane to Bien Hoa had already left, his orders were changed. He got reassigned to a
stateside base. He told my friend that had
we all missed that flight, we all would have
had our orders changed. Some guys just have
all the luck!

When we flew over the Great Lakes, I was
amazed at how big they were. I looked out of
the windows on both sides of the plane and
all I could see was water. At first I
thought we'd flown over the ocean. The
pilot made an announcement telling us that we
were flying over the Great Lakes shortly
after I'd looked out both sides so then I
knew for sure it wasn't the ocean.
Somewhere between New Jersey and Alaska we
were fed a meal. The stewardesses woke up
those who were sleeping and told everyone to
put our seats in the full upright position
and lower the tray from the back of the seat
in front of us. They always said it with a
smile so it was hard to get mad at them for
waking people up. I overheard one of my
fellow travelers say that they were fattening
us up for the slaughter like cattle at a feed
lot he'd seen. What a morbid comparison!

We landed at Anchorage, Alaska for fuel and
got a chance to leave the plane and walk
around a while and stretch our legs. There
wasn't much leg-room on a military charter
with 219 passengers aboard. It was freezing
cold out on the walk from the plane to the
terminal. They had no covered walkway connecting the plane to the terminal like they
had at most big airports. I was wearing
short-sleeved khaki 1505s to be ready for the

heat and humidity of Vietnam. I didn't know
there would be snow on the ground or that I'd
have to walk outside in it.

I saw a huge white Polar bear standing upright on a raised platform inside the terminal. It towered over all onlookers. I took a
picture of it and of the snow-covered mountains in the distance. This was my first
visit to Alaska and these were some of the
tallest snow-covered mountains I'd ever seen.

I bought a post card in the terminal gift
shop before reboarding the plane. It showed
Anchorage International Airport on the front.
On the back it said that it was called the
"Cross-roads of the World" because it served
the air traffic between the Orient and Europe.

It got dark shortly after taking off. We
were told that our next stop would be Yokota
Air Base, Japan. We were fed again somewhere
between Alaska and Japan. Most passengers,
including me, had been asleep and were awakened by the stewardesses. I didn't complain
because I was hungry and the food was good.

I couldn't see anything of Japan through
my window because it was very dark and sprink-
ling out when we landed. This was our last
refueling stop and we waited inside of the
passenger terminal while the plane was re-
fueled.

I looked around the gift shop and bought
another post card. This one had a picture of
the Heian Shrine in Kyoto on the front. On
the back it said the shrine was a replica of
the old Imperial palace buildings. It was
built in 1895 in commemoration of the 1,000th
anniversary of founding Kyoto as the capital
of ancient Japan.

We got back on the plane and most passengers went to sleep shortly after takeoff. I
lost track of time, having traveled through
so many different time zones and crossing the
international date line as well. Needless to
say, it was a very long trip.

I fell asleep shortly after leaving Japan.
Somewhere between Japan and Vietnam they woke
us up to eat another meal. One thing is for
sure, Uncle Sam wasn't going to send his men
off to war hungry. I found that it was
easier for me getting back to sleep with a
full stomach.

Sometime after I'd fallen asleep, I was
rudely awakened by someone screaming. Once
awake, I was scared and my heart was racing
because I thought we were going to crash.
Why else would someone be screaming in the
middle of the night on a passenger plane? I
soon found out why.

A soldier sitting only a couple of rows in
front of me was having a nightmare. He was
returning to Vietnam for a second tour of
duty and some pretty bad things happened on
his first tour. The guy sitting next to him
and a stewardess were talking to him, trying
to calm him down. After he was fully awake
and settled down, he apologized to the people
around him for waking them up.

I couldn't go back to sleep right away
after that incident. I was hoping that I
wouldn't end up like him in the future, having nightmares about stuff in Vietnam and
screaming about it in the middle of the night
and waking up other people. It was bad
enough that the VC (Viet Cong) could kill you
in Vietnam but they could try to kill you in
your dreams after you left Vietnam too.

When the pilot announced that we were
about to land at Bien Hoa Air Base, I looked
out the window. The only lights I saw were
those on the base when we got close to it.
The countryside all around it was totally
dark. He told us the local time and the tem-
perature. Then he reminded us to take all of
our stuff with us. After that, he wished us
good luck.

Shortly after the engines were off, the
front and back doors of the plane were opened. It started to get hot and humid real

quick. When the engines turned off, so did
the air conditioning. An Air Force sergeant
stepped into the aisle and introduced himself and welcomed us to Bien Hoa Air Base,
Republic of Vietnam.

I'd never seen a uniform like his before.
It was a different shade of green than the
fatigues I'd been issued in basic training,
with much larger pockets too. His shirt had
four large pockets with flaps and mine had
only one with no flaps. Instead of blue and
white stripes for rank on his upper sleeve,
his stripes were black and green, as were
his cloth name tag and Air Force tag. At
that moment I wondered if I'd get issued fatigues like that. When mine were ironed
with lots of starch, they were shiney. His
looked ironed but there was no starchy shine
to them.

As all the passengers got off the plane,
the stewardesses and flight crew said goodbye to each person. They wished us good
luck and said they hoped to fly us home next
year. I hoped they did too.

The humidity had an immediate impact on
me as soon as I left the plane. I was sweating a lot and I noticed the air had a different smell to it. I didn't know if jet
engine fumes had anything to do with it or
not. It was not a pleasant odor and I heard
several people ask, "What's that smell?"

There were two long lines of people
stretching from the plane to the terminal.
The sergeant that had welcomed us to Vietnam
told us in a loud voice so everyone could
hear, in case of attack, we should duck down
behind the wall that separated the flightline
from the terminal and also the wall just inside the terminal for those at the front of
the line. Both walls had been reinforced
with waist-high slabs of concrete, lined end-
to-end. About that time, a parachute flare
lit up the night from the other side of the
runway, several hundred yards away. I

tensed up, never having seen one before except for on TV and in the movies. Those
flares had a different affect on people when
seen in person in a war zone.

The line I was in moved slowly. As I got
closer to the terminal, I looked up over my
head. In between two entrance doorways was a
big dark blue sign with large white capital
letters that spelled out: CLEAR-ALL-WEAPONS.
Below the sign and on the ground was a 55-
gallon metal container painted bright red.
It was leaning outward with its opening away
from the terminal wall, held up at an angle
by a wooden frame. As I walked past it, I
could see that it was almost totally full of
sand. I thought I knew what it was for and
some time later someone told me and confirmed
what I'd thought. Guns with live ammo were
brought into this building every day.

An even larger sign on the same wall,
printed in blue, white and yellow capital
letters spelled out: DETACHMENT 5, 8TH
AERIAL PORT SQUADRON WELCOMES YOU TO BIEN HOA
AIR BASE REPUBLIC OF VIETNAM. Below that
portion of the sign, printed in blue on a
white background was: HOME OF THE 6251st AIR
BASE SQUADRON.

Over the front entrance of the terminal,
at the leading edge of a porch-like awning,
was a very big sign which read: DET. 5, 8th
AERIAL-PORT-SQUADRON PASSENGER TERMINAL BIEN
-HOA AB RVN in white letters on a blue background. I didn't see that one until the
next day.

The passenger terminal was a large light
tan metal building with a metal roof. It had
no doors on any of the outer walls. The two
sides on the narrow ends of the rectangular-
shaped building were wide open. There were
steel beams at these ends, with no walls.
The front side had only one entrance, a very
wide one with no doors. The rear of the terminal faced the flightline and it had several entrances, none with doors. Only the

offices inside of the terminal had doors and
wall-mounted air conditioners. The main
part of the terminal contained hundreds of
aluminum-framed multi-colored plastic seats
arranged in many rows. There were also many
rows of ceiling fans mounted over those
seats to help circulate the hot humid air.

The OIC (Officer-In-Charge) of the term-
inal had an office in the terminal as did
Customs, run by the Army MPs (Military Po-
lice). There was a Lost and Found Baggage
section, a DV (Distinguished Visitor)
Lounge, Tri-Service ATCO (Air Transportation
Coordinating Office), Passenger Processing
Section office and the Pacific Stars and
Stripes news stand.

The snack bar was located in a separate
building to the left side of the front main
entrance of the passenger terminal. The
latrines (restrooms) were also in a separate
building to the right of the front main entrance of the passenger terminal.

Arriving passengers would go to one of the
open ends of the building to collect their
bags. At the opposite end, also open with
no walls, was where people would check their
bags in when departing on a flight from Bien
Hoa. Only those passengers leaving here on
Air America flights or on helicopters would
not check their bags in at this end of the
terminal. They would keep their bags with
them all the time.

Once everyone from my flight was inside
the terminal, representatives from each
branch of the military divided us up into
different areas to sit. It was plain to see
that the Army had many more people than the
rest and that was to be expected.

The Air Force representative asked us to
raise our hands if we had orders to Bien Hoa
and if we did, to give him a copy. Even if
more than one of us was on a set of orders,
each one of us had to give him a copy. The
majority of Air Force people on my flight

had orders assigning them to Bien Hoa. We had
attended tech school together. Some of our
classmates would be arriving later on a flight
from Travis Air Force Base, California. We
were given a break to use the restroom and
collect our baggage, then we had to return to
the same area.

The group I was with was going to get a
ride to the VAQ (Visiting Airman Quarters),
sort of like a base hotel for the lowest
ranking people. Most of us had two pieces of
baggage to carry. Everyone had a green
duffle bag that was issued in basic training.
They were crammed full of mostly military
clothing and were very heavy. We also had a
small carry-on bag or briefcase that held our
travel orders, shot records, shaving gear,
cameras, and stuff like that.

A big truck pulled up at the baggage collection end of the terminal. We were told to
load up with our stuff in the back of it.
The two-and-a-half ton green truck with a
canvas cover over the back was called a
deuce-and-a-half. Nobody had thought to let
the tailgate down so it was a big climb up.
We sat on long wooden bench-style seats on
both sides of the truck bed, facing eachother with our baggage in front of our feet.

There was a big pile of stuff up at the
front end of the truck bed. With the canvas
top up, it was too dark for me to see what it
was. The staff sergeant who'd briefed us
earlier was sitting back there with us and he
told the guys sitting closest to the pile of
stuff to start passing out the pile of flak
jackets and helmets. He said to make sure
that each one of us got one of each. That's
how I found out what that pile of stuff was.
Then we were told to put them on and to sign
a form that was being passed around on a
clipboard. Those protective items were ours
to keep until we left Bien Hoa at the end of
our tours.

As we were driven across the base in the
back of the deuce-and-a-half, some of the

guys said out loud what I'd been thinking to
myself. We looked like the guys we'd seen in
war movies or TV shows. The main difference
being, we were in the Air Force and the guys
on TV or in the movies were either in the
Army or were Marines. We'd never seen Air
Force personnel wearing helmets and flak
jackets on TV or in any movie. These things
were heavy and hot and we took them off at
the first opportunity. They weren't worn
again until the base came under attack.

We were assigned two people to a room at
the VAQ. It was already past midnight when
we got there and we were going to be awakened at 6 a.m. I had not slept well on the
long trip getting here. The room air conditioner was a bit noisy but I was grateful
for the cool dry air it provided. I managed
to get to sleep my first night in Vietnam
without too much trouble.

Early in the morning of our first full
day "in-country", we piled into the back of
the deuce-and-a-half and were driven to the
chow hall. It's been called many different
things: dining facility, mess hall, Airman
Open Mess, chow hall. We called it the chow
hall then.

After a decent breakfast, our next stop
was our unit's orderly room. There we
officially signed in as "ready for duty" and
no longer were in "travel status." We were
introduced to TSgt (Technical Sergeant/E-6)
Marvin L. Denison, First Sergeant of Detachment 5, 8th Aerial Port Squadron. Then we
met our commander, Lieutenant Colonel
Crutchfield. He interviewed everyone in my
group, one person at a time. He asked me
what I'd been doing prior to enlisting in
the Air Force. I remember telling him that
I'd been a student at West Georgia College
in Carrollton, Georgia.

When my group left the orderly room, we
rode to our next destination in a 29-pass-
enger bus. It was Air Force blue and didn't

have any air conditioning or wire screens
over the windows like the big green Army
buses had. We opened all the windows because
of the heat and humidity.

Our next stop was the Aerial Port Squadron
barracks. Every unit had their own designated barracks. They all looked the same.
They were two story wooden buildings with tin
roofs, built in the shape of a capital letter
H. The center part contained the showers on
one side of the hall with sinks and toilets
on the opposite side. Both long sides of the
H contained the individual rooms, with some
buildings having a unit bar and recreation
room with pool table, card tables and a bar
with stools. Also, some buildings had supply
rooms at each end of both sides of the H and
at both ends were the exit/entrance doors
and steps connecting the upper floor to the
ground.

At ground level around the entire wooden
structure were thick slabs of concrete leaning against the outside walls. These were
for the protection of the occupants from
shrapnel, bullets, and exploding mortars and
122mm rockets. Of course if any of those
devices penetrated the corregated tin roof
and exploded inside of the barracks, then
somebody was going to be killed or wounded.

We were shown around the building that
would become our new home, beginning with the
top floor. It was empty now because as
people left the unit for a new assignment,
those rooms were left empty and as first
floor rooms became available for the same
reason, people living upstairs were moved
downstairs. We were told that anything we
found there could be kept and scrounging for
wood and nails and other building supplies
was encouraged. We'd soon find out why.

The top floor would soon be boarded up and
all of us new guys would occupy the ground
floor rooms. We were told it was because it
was safer living on the ground floor. The
shelter just outside of our barracks was

condemned and boarded up because it was literally falling apart. So in case of an
attack on the base, we were to put our helmets and flak jackets on, crawl under our
beds, and get close to the outer wall of the
building since it was protected by those big
concrete slabs on the other side of it.

While looking around upstairs, I found a
small crossbow, like the one I'd seen used in
the movie The Green Berets. We were all surprised that the arrow I shot into the wall
stuck in it while I was trying to see just
how powerful the crossbow was. That little
wooden arrow would have gone through a person easily. Somebody told me that I should
keep the crossbow for self-defense in case
our barracks came under a sapper attack. I
ended up giving it away when I found out it
was illegal to have one. Some people kept
things like this whether they were legal or
not.

We were then shown around the ground
floor portion of the barracks. The part that
we were going to live in appeared to be only
partially built. There were wooden beams and
braces here and there but no walls along the
hall or to separate the long open spaces into
separate rooms.

The staff sergeant who was in charge of
our group marked off what he estimated was
enough space for a room for two people and
then we were paired off until there were
three of us left. Initially we were told
that two of us would have a room and one of
us would room alone. That's how it was in
the beginning.

We were given saws, hammers, crowbars and
nails and then given the rest of the day off
to build our own rooms within the barracks.
We scrounged around for beds, wall lockers
and everything else we needed and ended up
with a decent room arrangement. John
Karasek and I shared a room and Armand
Fecteau was our neighbor, at least initially.

Over the next few weeks we put up some unusual decorations. As long as we didn't display anything offensive, it was alright. We
were mainly just trying to cover up either
bare walls without paint on them or walls
that had paint but that looked bad in some
way. Big posters we'd found were used a lot
because paint was in short supply at the
time.

We had our first room inspection shortly
after finishing our room-building project.
Our commander and first sergeant did an in-
formal walk-through. Room inspections were
common in the military in 1971, even in Vietnam.

One day John, Armand and I discussed how
we could improve upon our room situation.
We agreed to move the bunkbed that John and
I slept on into the other room that held
Armand's single bed. We also moved our two
wall lockers into that room as well, intend-
ing to make that into a bedroom. My former
room would then be turned into a livingroom.

To complete the room transformation, we
cut a small doorway in the wall that separated the two rooms so we could walk directly
from one room to the other and not have to
walk into the hallway to get from one room
to the other as before.

We found some plastic chairs and put them
in the livingroom. Then we built some overhead cabinets to store food and other things
in. We also made a desk so we'd have a
place to sit when we wrote letters home. We
also bought a small refrigerator at the BX
(Base Exchange). We stocked it with soft
drinks and juice and bought some food items
to keep handy so if we didn't want to walk
to the chow hall in the pouring rain, we
could eat here and stay dry.

More days of in-processing followed. Remember, this was 1971, a long time before
personal computers and automation in the
military. We had to hand-carry a list of

all the places we had to go to get a signature from someone at each place on the list
and give each office a copy of our travel
orders. This took up a lot of time, especially when we had to walk to a lot of
those places. At some of those in-processing appointments, we had to listen to some
kind of briefing or go on a tour somewhere.

At the Accounting and Finance Office,
they told me that my pay records weren't
there and they couldn't pay me. Just great,
I thought. Here I am in Vietnam where I
could get killed and I'm not even old enough
to vote, not old enough to buy a beer and
not going to get paid either! For awhile I
had to live on what little I came here with.

We all went to CBPO (Consolidated Base
Personnel Office) where we filled out some
forms. We also went to the post office and
received our addresses and combination-type
P.O. boxes. Then we went to the base chapel
and the library. Later at the base headquarters building, a briefing officer showed
us a 122mm Russian-made rocket on display.
It was over six feet tall! We left that
building with some reading material about
the base.

I finally got some time to sit down and
write a few lines on the postcard I'd
bought in Alaska. I didn't want my parents
worrying about me. I mailed it the next day
without putting a stamp on it. Our mail
from Vietnam required no postage. We were
told to write the word FREE over the spot
where a stamp would normally go.

The next day I got a chance to write
again, using the postcard I'd bought in
Japan. My address was: AMN Steve Crews FR
(Social Security number went after the FR)
                    Det. 5, 8 APSQ (PACAF)
                    APO San Francisco 30227
Back then, social security numbers were
required on just about everything in the
military, on mail, uniforms, medical records

and any form that had your name on it. Nobody had any identity theft problems then.
Ah, the good old days!

There was a water fountain in the hall
near the latrine and showers. I took a
drink from it the first day I saw it. The
water was nice and cold but tasted horrible,
the way water stored in an old rusty container might taste. That first taste of
water from there was also my last. I guess
rusty pipes were the cause of the foul-tast-
ing water. I doubt if I drank more than one
gallon of plain water my whole year in Vietnam. As long as the BX had a supply of
sodas and the snack bar and chow hall had
other things to drink, I stayed hydrated.

One interesting place we "newbees" (FNGs
in Army slang) were taken to during our
first week at Bien Hoa was the Apollo Club.
It was an old French hotel on the Vietnamese
side of the base. Americans occupied half
of the base, Vietnamese the other half.
There was no physical divider that I can recall. The Apollo Club was where we got our
introduction to the world of Vietnamese bar
girls. We soon found out the difference between a "ladies drink" which was also called
"Saigon tea" and a beer. The difference was
that if you bought a bar girl a ladies
drink, it cost about twice as much as your
own, and their drink was non-alcoholic
"Saigon tea."
Nobody there checked IDs so even the
youngest in our group could buy a beer. Nobody cared if we were 21 or not. As soon as
we sat down, a bar girl would squeeze into
the booth next to you and ask, "You buy me
drink?"
The bar girls in the club used American
names like Suzy, Jane, Sherry, Linda, etc.,
instead of their real names. They weren't
very pretty in my opinion, although the

younger ones could pass for "cute." They all
used too much perfume, too much makeup and
their breath smelled awful from the nuoc mam
sauce made from fermented fish parts they
liberally applied to some of their food. The
odor of nuoc mam is detectable at a long distance by those of us new to Vietnamese
culture. The odor remains for many hours
after eating; worse than garlic.

Since the city of Bien Hoa was off-limits
to all military personnel, the Apollo Club
attracted some people to its offerings. Its
main attractions were alcohol, including
Vietnamese "33" beer (also called tiger piss
by some), music and women. The club offered
a change in scenery from the barracks if nothing else. The bar girls spoke some
English but their conversations usually cen-
tered around "You buy me drink?", "You beau
coup dinkai dau!" (You very crazy), or "You
numba ten GI!" Number ten is bad while
number one is very good. If you didn't buy
them a drink, they thought you were a cheap
numba ten GI. I was one of those.

Another stop on our tour of the base was
a business not far from our barracks. It
was a combination of souvineer stand, tailor
shop and a French-built steam bath house,
also known as a massage parlor. It was located in one corner of the American side of
the base, next to the Cambodian compound by
the outside perimeter fence and within short
walking distance of our barracks, which was
very convenient. Many GIs stationed at Bien
Hoa bought "boonie" hats from them if they
weren't issued by their units and then had
the tailor shop sew on patches that were
bought there. They also sold a wide variety
of metal pins and their prices were very
reasonable.

I bought my "boonie" hat there and still
have it after all these years. I had a large

patch sewn on the top which had the words
"Peace, Love" and around the outside I put on
some pins that said, "Power to the People",
"Viet Cong Hunting Club" and also a Playboy
Bunny pin. I had a peace flag sewn on one
side and a Confederate battle flag on the
other. On the front I had a cloth patch
sewn on. It had the words "Bien Hoa AB,
Republic of Vietnam." Later in my tour I
added a two-star general's silver stars and
painted them white and I put them on the
front over the Bien Hoa AB patch.

There were a couple of daring people in
my squadron, including myself, who wore
peace flag pins on the corner of their uniform shirt lapels while at work. I thought
they were being tolerated for morale pur-
poses. One night at work I was asked to
keep my peace flag pin out of sight. I com-
plied by removing it from the outside of my
lapel and re-positioned it under the lapel,
out of sight. The Paris Peace Talks were
going on at the time and I thought that I
was showing my support for peace. Wasn't it
President Nixon, my Commander-In-Chief who
said he'd get us "peace with honor?" I was
all for that! I just wasn't allowed to
support that viewpoint on my uniform.
    Multi-colored cloth headbands with "Viet-
nam" printed on them were popular things to
wear on the flightline. I bought one of
those too but only wore it a few times. If
you saw any of the Rambo movies, the head-
band he wore, at least in the way that he
wore it, is what I'm talking about. They
had no elastic band to hold them in place.
You tied it around your head with a knot at
the back where the extra material hung down.
They were tolerated along with colored beads
worn as necklaces and sunglasses of various
colors. Some black military members wore
wristbands made of cloth or leather that had
green, black and red wide bands of colors.

The Cambodians who lived next to the souvineer stand and tailor shop had their own
private compound, built inside a strong defensive position with lots of barbed wire,
concrete walls, bunkers, and machine gun
positions everywhere it seemed. Our group
of in-processing "newbees" got to visit inside of that place once. It was normally
off-limits to us but one day we were de-
tailed to deliver some supplies to them with
a deuce-and-a-half truck. Extra details
were a way of life then.

The people who lived there had been
trained to fight by the U.S. Army's Detachment A-303 of the Special Forces. The armed Cambodian's official name was Forces
Armees Nationales Khmer. They wore dark
camo-fatigues and black berets. Their
American advisors and trainers wore green
berets. Their families lived inside of the
compound with them.

That was the first time in my life that
I'd seen babies walking around with shirts
on but no pants or diapers. They just used
the ground whenever they had to go to the
bathroom. The way they lived, the world was
their toilet. No wonder the air there always had a funky smell to it.

We were told that they were here because
their original homes in Cambodia had been
overrun by the Communist Vietnamese and Cambodians and these people fled to join other
free Cambodians in South Vietnam to regroup
and fight again. The combined force of U.S.
and Cambodian military forces here were
known as the Mobile Guerilla Force.

Their living quarters were like old wood-
en open-bay barracks of World War II vintage
with few furnishings. Most of them slept on
mats on the floor and what few individual
rooms existed had walls made of cardboard
and paper. They cooked over open flames
outside and had community-style outhouses

for everyone except the babies to use as their
bathroom. I saw babies being breast-fed and
lots of little kids running around bare-footed
and bare-bottomed. The adult's clothes were
light and silky, dark colored and usually only
men wore shoes or boots. Most of the Cambodian men I saw were in uniform and carried
weapons. I don't remember if they had M-16s
or AK-47s. I just remember seeing lots of
guns.

The Army sergeant that gave us a quick tour
of the place said that the Cambodians and
Vietnamese didn't get along with eachother
and that's why they lived in their own separate compound. They were ancient enemies going back many centuries.

Those of us who lived nearby were glad to
have them close by in case of a major ground
attack against the base. Those people were
well-trained fighters, well-armed and well-
led. They may have been living a primitive
lifestyle compared to ours but they had my
respect. They were willing to fight for
their freedom.

Another place we were taken to see during
our in-processing and base orientation were
the dog kennels. On the opposite side of the
flightline from where we worked, the SPs (Air
Force Security Police) had a large dog
kennel where their German Shepard dogs were
trained and lived. On the way there, we
passed by an old A-1 Skyraider that had crash-
landed into the barbed wire perimeter near
the base garbage dump only a quarter of a
mile from the dog kennels.

We were told that during the big Communist
Tet Offensive in 1968, hundreds of enemy
forces were killed along the barbed wire perimeter by old Korean War-era propeller-
driven A-1 Skyraiders. They bombed and
strafed the enemy all around American defensive positions. This plane was shot down and

didn't quite make it back to the runway which
was only a short distance away. I don't know
why it was left there. It was rusting away
in the spot where it had crashed, a vivid re-
minder of the war going on all around us.

As we approached the dog kennels for a
closer look, the large barking German Shepards were all up and looking fierce and
aggressive. I didn't get within five feet of
their fence because they kept jumping up
against it trying to get at us. They looked
like tigers who hadn't eaten in a week. Some
of them were trained to sniff out drugs, some
were trained to detect explosives and the
majority were trained as guard dogs, used to
attack and overpower intruders. It was easy
to imagine a ninety pound dog attacking a
ninety pound Viet Cong, tearing up the man
like a rag doll. Those dogs could do it too!

Once we got our rooms built in the barracks and completed the in-processing requirements, our training began. We were
taken around to the passenger terminal work-
centers and briefly told what type of work
was performed there. It seemed like most of
the offices wanted to know who could type.
I'd taken a typing class in high school, using only a manual typewriter. The ones in
use here were all electric so I kept my
mouth shut and was glad I did. One of the
guys in my group said he could type and he
got assigned to the Lost and Found Baggage
section. Every day he had to do a complete
inventory of every type of luggage or piece
of clothing brought there and that included
opening the luggage and doing an inventory
of all the contents. He did a lot of typing.
His office had no windows but it did have a
wall air conditioner so at least he worked
in comfort. Still, twelve hours of inven-
tories and typing, ugh!

Little of what we were taught in tech

school was put to any use here. In the Passenger Service operations, only military, no
dependents or other civilians except for the
USO shows passing through, were processed for
flights from here to anywhere else.

Some of us, myself included, were trained
to drive 29 and 45 passenger buses, 4K, 10K
and 10K AT (All Terrain) forklifts, warehouse
tugs, mobile baggage conveyor, 3-ton highlift
truck and how to position the aircraft boarding steps which were towed behind the warehouse tugs. They were basically heavy-duty
metal steps on a strong metal frame that
rolled on wheels.
I volunteered to tow the boarding steps
with a warehouse tug mainly because a lot of
the stewardesses on the DC-8s and B-707s
(civilian airlines contracted with the Department of Defence to transport military
personnel to and from Vietnam) would give us
bags of leftover hot ham and cheese sand-
wiches, cups of fruit cocktail, and small
containers of real milk. Somebody had advised me to never volunteer for anything
over here but of course this was an excep-
tion that I was glad I made. I always shared these goodies with my friends. We all
appreciated what we were given by the stewardesses.   Their acts of kindness really
gave a boost to our morale.

The barracks I was assigned to wasn't air
conditioned. I bought a small rotating fan
in the BX and at night I'd put it on a chair
at the foot of my bed. When I put my mosquito net down for the night, the fan had to
be right up next to the net in order to feel
any air circulating. The humidity in the
room was always high and the fan made it a
little easier to deal with.

One night I decided to read the hand-out

given to us during our in-processing. It explained a lot of things about the base.

BIEN HOA AIR BASE
Welcome to Bien Hoa Air Base. Located
approximately 18 miles northeast of Saigon,
and formerly one of the busiest airports in
the world, the base is the headquarters for
the United States Air Force's 6251st Air Base
Squadron. It is also the home of the Vietnamese Air Force's (VNAF) Air Logistics Command (ALC) and 3rd Air Division.
U.S. activities at this installation are
being turned over to the VNAF on a planned
schedule commensurate with the goals of the
Improvement and Modernization (I & M) or
Vietnamization Program. For this reason you
will probably be working in or notice sections with integrated USAF/VNAF personnel
staffs. The same applies to many of the operational and maintenance facilities, many
of which have already converted to joint-use
status. No date has been announced for complete base closure or USAF forces with-
drawal.
Two USAF flying units remain from an operational combat air force at one time composed of five units. They are the 8th
Special Operations Squadron, one of the Air
Force's oldest fighter squadrons, and a task
force of the 19th Tactical Air Support
Squadron, the headquarters of which is located at Phan Rang AB, RVN.
The 8th SOS, the only operational USAF
squadron in Southeast Asia equipped with
A-37B Dragonfly jet attack fighters, supports
both Military Regions 3 and 4 from Bien Hoa
in operations against the enemy. The 19th
TASS task force, equipped with the OV-10 and
O-2A aircraft, provide forward air controller
(FAC) support for ground force operations.
The air base squadron, formerly the
6251st Combat Support Group and redesignated

a squadron as of 1 September 1971, is com-
prised of eight sections: headquarters, security police, transportation, supply, dispensary, munitions, transient alert and the aerospace ground equipment (AGE) section.

Other units at Bien Hoa include: 6005th
Support Squadron, 8th Aerial Port Squadron,
1877th Communications Squadron, 834th Air
Division, OLG-1st Weather Group, 37th Aerospace Rescue and Recovery Squadron (FOL), 3rd
Aerospace Rescue and Recovery Group (Det. 6),
OSI (Det. 5005), 6499th Special Activities,
483rd Tactical Airlift Wing (OL), 6250th Support Group, 1505th Postal, and 4384th Audi-
tor General (Det.).

In addition to the above units there are
Air Force Advisory Teams (AFAT) 3 and 6.
These teams work with the VNAF operational
and logistics units. The VNAF maintain and
fly the A-1 Skyraider which is a reciprocat-
ing engine fighter-bomber; the F-5 Freedom
Fighter, a supersonic twin-jet aircraft; O-1
Bird Dog and UH-1H Huey helicopters. Their
mission is to provide close air support for
Vietnamese and Free World ground forces.

GENERAL INFORMATION

Military Courtesy - is observed at this
installation between officers and enlisted
men of the U.S. and other Free World Forces.
VNAF officers can be distinguished by the
silver or gold band on their headgear, plus
other insignia displayed on shirts and jackets, similar in appearance to the American
major and lieutenant colonel insignia.

Military Pay - All personnel are paid
once a month on the last day of the month.
Payment is by check or Military Payment
Certificates (MPC). MPC may be converted to
Vietnamese Piasters on base. The official
rate of conversion is 275 piasters to the
dollar. American paper money is not used and
it is considered an offense for an individual

to possess it beyond 24 hours after entering
the country or receiving said currency.
Under new regulations, all pay, except sub-
sistance allowances, may be allotted to a de-
pendant, bank, or savings institution. Personnel are encouraged to participate in the
10% Savings Deposit Plan. U.S. Savings
Bonds may be cashed in U.S. branch banks in
the Republic of Vietnam.

   Passes and R & R - All personnel are eligible for R & R after serving three months
of their tour. Regular trips are scheduled
to: Hong Kong, Bangkok, Taipei, Honolulu and
Sydney. One seven-day R & R not charged as
leave is authorized during a tour. In addition, a special three-day "in-country"
R & R to China Beach (Da Nang) Vietnam, is
authorized.

   Off Limits Areas - All cities, towns and
villages, including Saigon, are off limits
to personnel stationed at Bien Hoa. Except
on official business or in transit. Personnel are not permitted to remain in Bien
Hoa City overnight. All Vietnamese depend-
ant quarters on Bien Hoa Air Base are off
limits unless personnel are specifically in-
vited into the quarters as bona fide guests.
Personnel on pass, leave, or visiting another area will be held responsible for com-
pliance with all policies established by the
area pertaining to off limits, curfew and
dress restrictions. When U.S. personnel ob-
serve civil disturbances or demonstrations
while enroute to or from Bien Hoa Air Base,
they will not become involved or participate
but will report to the nearest U.S. military unit.

   Base Library - A 11,000 - volume facility
is maintained with over 6,000 square feet of
floor space. Current periodicals, Sunday
issues of top stateside newspapers, tape recordings, phonograph records, hardbound and
pocket books are available to suit the most

varied of tastes in literature and art. The
library is open from 0800 to 2400 hours
daily. (Building #1504).

Postal Services - Post Office window hours
for registry are 0800 to 1100 and 1300 to
1700, Monday through Saturday; for money orders 0800 to 1100 and 1200 to 1600, Monday
through Saturday. Hours for parcel post and
stamps are 0800 to 1700, Monday through Saturday. There is one mail run a day for pick
up and delivery of mail.

Red Cross - There are three American Red
Cross representatives at Bien Hoa (phone
3911 or 3912). Office hours are 0730 to
1630 daily. Service is available 24 hours a
day for emergencies, after office hours dial
2251 for duty worker number. To assist military authorities in making a decision regarding a request for emergency leave the American Red Cross will initiate a request for
verification of circumstances through the
local home town Red Cross chapter. To ex-
pedite action, inform your family to immed-
iately contact the local chapter of the Red
Cross in any case in which the family feels
your presence is recommended because of an
emergency at home.

Religious Services - There are both Pro-
testant and Catholic chaplins. Services are
held throughout the day on Sunday. Other
activities are scheduled throughout the week.
A Jewish chaplin visits Bien Hoa regularly;
his visits are announced in the Daily Bulletin.

R & R Center, Building #1504 - One of the
more popular areas is the R & R Center, open
daily from 0730 to 1800. After 90 days in
country, one is eligible for a 7 day R & R to
one of five locations (Hawaii, Austrailia,
Bangkok, Hong Kong or Taipei). Also available is the new 7 & 7 leave program or 14
days leave back to the U.S. In addition, a 3
day R & R is available to China Beach near

Da Nang. All service and information can be obtained from the R & R Center.

The Hobby Shop, Building #1510 - The Base Hobby Shop contains fully equipped Photo Shop with facilities for developing black and white and ektachrome film, plus 12 enlarging stations. Another outstanding feature of the Hobby Shop is a 20 station Tape Center for the reproduction of more than 1500 musical selections to choose from. The Hobby Shop has a complete Lapidary Shop, Leather Shop, and a Slot Car Racing Area. Qualified instructors are on duty at all times to provide advice and assistance.

Consolidated Open Mess (COM) Building #2800 - The Officers Open Mess and the NCO Open Mess are consolidated in a single building and includes a Main Dining Room, an Officer's Lounge, an NCO Lounge, a Barber Shop, a game room in both the Officer's and NCO's Lounge, and check cashing facilities. Its hours of operation are from 0700 to 2300 hours Sunday through Friday and from 0700 to 2400 hours on Saturday. The specified hours for breakfast are 0700 to 0830 hours. Lunch is served from 1100 to 1330 hours and dinner is served from 1700 to 2130 hours. Entertainment is offered during the week with added floor shows twice a month.

The Airmen's Annex, Building #3000 - The Airmen's Club is operated as an annex to the COM and includes a cash checking facility, a lounge, a game room, a dining room, and a barber shop. Lunch and short orders are available from 1100 to 2130 hours. Entertainment is offered during the week with added floor shows twice a month. Hours of operation are from 1000-2200 hours Sunday through Friday. On Saturdays, the hours of operation are from 1000-2300 hours.

Base Gymnasium, Building #1465 - The Base Gymnasium is an excellent facility and includes an open-air court for basketball and

volleyball with lighting for night play.
League play goes on all year round. It also
houses a weight room with a wide variety of
body building and conditioning equipment.
There is an equipment issue room along with
locker and shower facilities available too.
A sauna room, one of the few in Vietnam, is
located in the Base Gym. The Gym's hours of
operation are from 1000 hours to 2400 hours,
7 days a week.

Swimming Pool Adjacent to Building #1465
Bien Hoa Air Base has a new outdoor swimming
pool 60' X 40' with a 1 meter diving board
and areas for relaxing in the sun. Adjacent
to the swimming pool is an enclosed picnic
area for cook-outs and picnics. Its hours
of operation are from 1000 hours to 2300
hours, 7 days a week.

Movies - The theater has a seating capacity of 325 and is air conditioned. It is
open 7 days a week with 5 to 6 showings a
day. This building is also used for USO
Shows and Commander's Calls.

Uniforms - Due to the climate and working conditions at Bien Hoa, either the short
or long sleeve fatigue uniform or 1505s are
worn. Blues are not worn because of the
year-round hot climate. Casual, summer
clothing of the wash and wear variety is recommended for off-duty wear. A sports
jacket should be brought for use on R & R.
The base exchange and several tailor shops
on base carry civilian garments. In addition, there is a well-stocked clothing sales
store.

Sanitation - Diarrhea is a common com-
plaint of Americans in South Vietnam. Do
not drink tap water or eat uncooked fresh
vegetables on the local economy. Peel all
locally purchased fruit. Do not use ice in
drinks bought in local establishments.
Bottled beverages for sale are potable.
This includes the local beers and soft

drinks. While on base, drink only water from the dining halls, open messes or approved water fountains. Water in latrines is not potable and should be used only for washing.

Educational Opportunities - The base education office is in building 1504. An advisor is on duty to provide assistance. Enrollment in high school, college and technical correspondence courses may be arranged. USAFI, ECI and Army technical courses are also available. Undergraduate college courses are offered on base by the University of Maryland. High school and college GED tests are also provided.

Dispensary - The Dispensary is located just north of the Finance Office. In and out-patient services for all military and civilian personnel are provided. Services include the Air Force Clinic, Flight Surgeon's Office, X-ray, laboratory, pharmacy, an 11 bed ward and preventive and veterinary medicine sections. In addition, hospitalization beyond the dispensary's ability is provided by two local Army hospitals and the 483rd USAF Dispensary at Cam Ranh Bay Air Base. Appointments at the Dispensary may be obtained by calling 3952.

Dental Clinic - The Dental Clinic is in the dispensary. Information on services and appointments can be obtained by phoning 3113.

Firearms - Privately owned firearms are prohibited in the Republic of Vietnam. Only government issued weapons will be used, and when authorized for retention in quarters will be properly secured and kept in good working condition. Firearms will be carried only when in uniform and on duty.

MARS - Telephone service to the United States is provided by the base MARS station. Next to the motor pool, it is open 24 hours a day. Calls are free to the point of contact in the United States; from that point

they are collect. Free MARS GRAMS are available. There is also a USO-sponsored commercial line available for calls three days a
week.

That was the entire hand-out given to me
during in-processing, exactly as the original
was with their capitalizations and spelling.
During my time at Bien Hoa, I went to each of
those places mentioned in the literature except for the Red Cross and MARS station.
Most of those places I went to just once to
satisfy my curiosity. I went to the gym and
swimming pool several times with friends and
I visited the clubs and movie theater a few
a few times too.

At different times during my year in Vietnam, I was given things to carry in my
wallet. I had an Installation Identification
Card which everyone had to keep on their person at all times. It had my name, social
security number, rank, organization, name and
rank of my commanding officer as well as his
phone number on it. I also had a Small Arms
Hand Receipt, which we referred to as our
"gun card." It had my name, rank, social
security number, organization, the word
RIFLE typed in the nominclature space, M-16
was typed in the model space, its serial number, COLT typed in the manufacturer space,
Butt no. 19, 90 rounds of ammo, 5 magazines,
date qualified, and was signed by the first
sergeant. At the time, TSgt Thomas Hayden
had replaced TSgt Marvin Denison as our
"first shirt."
I also received a U.S. Government Motor
Vehicle Operator's Identification Card, which
we all called a government driver's license.
VIETNAM was stamped on the front in black ink
and large block letters. Over the next ten
years I eventually was licensed to drive so
many different types and sizes of vehicles

that an additional form had to be added to
the original one because it didn't have the
space on it to list all the things I was
trained to drive.

Last, but not least, I was given a membership card to the Airmen's Club and later
in my tour got a membership card for the COM
(Consolidated Open Mess). Except for the
Airmen's Club card, I still have all of the
other ones. When they were all in my wallet, I had more forms of ID than I had money
to spend.

Other souvineers I brought back from
Vietnam include a Christmas card dated 1971,
showing the Bien Hoa Air Base chapel with a
Christmas menu printed inside. Also, two
passes authorizing me to travel to Long Binh
Army Base, two tape recordings of rocket
attacks made on Bien Hoa Air Base and two
photo albums full of pictures taken in
different places in Vietnam. I think the
best souvineers of all were the letters my
mother saved that I wrote from Vietnam.

After a long 12-hour day at work, my
roommates and some friends of ours would
get together in our living room for some
cold drinks and hot story telling. Most of
the stories were about what happened to us
during basic training or tech school.
There was a lot of talk about where everyone preferred to go for their R & R too.

Some of the guys who dropped by for a
visit had either been in my tech school
class or a class or two ahead of it: Coy
Elrod, William Newborg, Michael Desmuke,
Willie Wells, Francis Barner, Michael Seft,
Thomas Shreve, Alvin Howard, Martin Vetter,
Thomas Job, Christopher Montero, Patrick
Baugh, Scott Pippert, James Staudenraus,
Gary Hayes, Paul Aguilar, and of course my
two roommates, Armand Fecteau and John
Karasek. Coincidentally, everyone I just

named got promoted to A1C (Airman First
Class, E-3, two stripes in the Air Force) the
same day I did, effective 1 February 1972.   I
still have a copy of those promotion orders.
I would run into Scott Pippert, Alvin Howard
and SSgt Chris Smith later in my career.

I was told that our unit at Bien Hoa had
one of the highest rates for VD (venereal
disease, now days called STDs, sexually
transmitted disease).   It also had a bad
drug problem.   I remember walking between
barracks sometimes and seeing small glass
vials on the ground that once contained
heroin.   Opium and marijuana were easy to
get too.
One of the guys who'd arrived at Bien Hoa
around the time I did was sent back to the
States after being here for only a few
weeks.   One day, everyone in our detachment,
at that time slightly over two hundred
people, was called to take part in a mass
urinalysis test and it was discovered that
this guy had a detectable amount of drugs in
his system.
We'd only been here a couple of weeks
when all of us new guys (FNGs in Army slang)
were taken by bus to a drug rehabilitation
center run by the Army.   The place consisted
of a few wall tents surrounded by a barbed
wire fence in the 1st Cavalry Division camp
on the other side of the flightline from the
Air Force part of the air base.
An Army spokesperson there gave us warn-
ings about the serious dangers involved
with drug use.   We were even told by some of
the rehabilitating drug users themselves
about the bad effects they'd experienced and
the problems caused by their drug usage.   It
messed up their personal lives and their
military careers.   Whether it was opium or
marijuana, the patients said that it only
made their lives more miserable, especially

if they got busted and their families found out.

Most of the patients we saw wore hospital robes and slippers and they looked very pale and skinny. Also, most of them had gone the "cold turkey" route of detoxification and cure from drug addiction and it caused them a lot of physical suffering. They looked a lot older than their actual ages. In short, they looked like hell and they said they felt like it too. I sure didn't want to end up like any of them. This "field trip" had a lasting affect on me. I never bought any drugs in Vietnam, even though they were cheap and easy to get.

On October 27, 1971, a very heavy rain caused my room in the barracks to become flooded with a couple of inches of water. After work, John and I borrowed a shovel from someone and dug a ditch near the outside wall of our room. It would chanel the flow of water away from the door at the end of the hall where the water had flowed in. We also put sandbags all along the outside of that same wall. We never got flooded again after that. As soon as it stopped raining, the mosquitos started flying again. I don't know how they survived the heavy rains, but they did.

Our Mama-san collected $4.00 each month from all of us. I was surprised at how cheaply it was to live here and not have to do all the things for ourselves that we had to do back in the States. Mama-san shined our shoes, washed and ironed all our clothes and swept the floor. She even made up our beds! We provided her with shoe polish and soap in addition to the $4.00 but that was still a great bargain for us.

Each day at work I was noticing how use-

less our Air Force tech school had been. It
was a huge waste of our time and tax-payer
dollars. They could have sent us all here as
DDAs (Direct Duty Assignees) and taught us
our jobs here using the OJT (On-The-Job-
Training) method, which is what happened
after we got here anyway. I worked the 7 a.m.
to 7p.m.shift and was told that I'd be moved
to the 7p.m.to 7a.m.shift. What was frustrating for me was they wouldn't tell me exactly when I'd be changing shifts. Every
couple of weeks they'd tell me again that it
would happen but they weren't sure just when.

One night some friends and I met in the
detachment bar. There were six or seven of
us who had gone through tech school together
and after having a drink, went outside to a
nearby basketball court. It was situated in
between the base perimeter road and the last
barracks in a short row of them that belonged to our unit.
We sat around in a circle on the cement
court. Somebody had brought a bottle of wine
outside with them and passed it around for
all to share. We were talking about our new
jobs and things and everyone was getting a
taste of the wine. After the bottle had
been passed around our circle of friends a
few times, the group started to mellow out.
Guys started laughing at most anything being
said whether it was funny or not.
To make things even livelier, some parachute flares had been fired high up over the
large open field across the road from us,
outside of the base perimeter barbed wire
fences. That turned our little get-together
a little brighter and gave us something else
to talk about and to laugh at. For some
reason, I still don't know why, the parachute
flares had us in a laughing uproar. I became convinced that night that laughter was
truely contagious!

We must have gotten pretty loud because
somebody stuck their head out of the bar
door and asked, "What the hell is going on?"
A member of our group pointed up at the
parachute flare that was lighting up the
night sky and told him we were laughing at
the "cool fireworks display." We were asked
to quiet down before the SPs (Security
Police) showed up and arrested us for being
drunk and disorderly. The "basketball court
gang" got much quieter after that, no thanks
to some of the guys who were holding a
finger up to their lips going "Ssshhh!"
loudly for all to hear, and giggling as they
did so. What a night!

Little get-togethers like that were held
from time to time but, unlike that night, we
managed to keep the noise level down and under control. We didn't want to get into any
trouble even though one guy said, "What are
they going to do, send us to Vietnam?" I
had to laugh at that!

CHAPTER TWO

NOVEMBER 1971

By November 1st, I'd worked without assistance or supervision for the first time. I got to drive a 10K forklift too and was complimented on my ability to set cargo pallets down on three-point dunnage quicker than the other trainees. That ability would come in handy later in my tour.

I was starting to get used to working 12 hours a day too. My first stretch at work lasted nine days and then I got my first day off. Then I worked eight days and got another day off. After that, we were on a 6 and 1 schedule, working six days and then getting a day off. I know that there were lots of military personnel in Vietnam who had it much tougher than I did and they have my respect, even if they did refer to guys working on main bases as REMFs. (Rear Echelon Mike Foxtrots). I'm just telling what my own experiences were.

My first job was in the Tri-Service ATCO (Air Transportation Coordinating Office) office, just inside the main entrance to the passenger terminal. It was a small office with a big plexiglass window with two slots cut out of it at about waist level. On the inside was a counter top at which we could either stand up or sit down on a stool to do our work. It reminded me of a movie theater box office where you bought your tickets. The entrance door was on the side near the front entrance to the terminal. There was one desk, one safe, one couch and two stools in the office. MTAs (Military Travel Authorizations) were kept in the safe. These were similar to airline tickets. You had to have one of these light blue forms in order to get on a commercial airliner to fly

from here back to the States. MTAs were
valuable documents and that's why we had to
keep them in the safe.

My first supervisor was a deep-voiced
Texan, A1C (Airman First Class) Harvey
Othell "Oh Hell" Davis. He told me that he
was trying to cross train into a radio
announcer job and he certainly had the voice
for it. He was leaving soon on a 30-day
leave and then return to Vietnam for a second tour. Therefore, he didn't have a lot
of time to train me, so I had to catch on
quickly, which I did.

He introduced me to the Vietnamese secretary. Her name was Thuy Van. I thought
that she was very pretty. I'd seen only a
few Vietnamese women on the base and they
were nowhere near as good looking as she was
in my opinion. She spoke English well but
with an accent that took me awhile to get
used to. She taught me a few Vietnamese
words and phrases. Her job was to do any
typing that needed to be done.

There was only one airman working in the
ATCO office when I got there. He was about
to return to the states to be discharged
from the Air Force. That was another reason
they wanted me to learn the job quickly.
Everyone there was leaving! Before he left,
he told me he needed some cash and offered
me a good deal on some long-playing vinyl
record albums and a stereo system. It had a
turntable, cassette tape player, AM & FM
radio all under a dust cover, along with two
speakers. Back in 1971, those were very popular.

Initially, my primary job was to make
announcements on the PA (Public Address) system and tell passengers about flights leaving
Bien Hoa at certain times, where they were
going and how many seats were available for
passengers.

For the in-country flights on military

aircraft like C-130s, passengers would bring
me a copy of their travel orders and I'd
write the information I needed on flight information forms, like their names, rank,
branch of service, stuff like that. I turned
in the completed forms and travel orders to
another office where they prepared the passenger manifests.

The next step was to tell the passengers
where to check in their bags and what time
they'd be boarding their flight. Somebody
else would later make announcements directing the passengers where to go to get on
flight number such and such going to places
like Da Nang or Cam Ranh Bay or Vung Tau for
example. For passengers on Emergency Leave
status, if they didn't have time to get
their MTA from TMO (Transportation Manage-
ment Office), we had to type up their blank
MTA form we kept in our safe and then they'd
turn it in at the check-in counter where they
also checked in their luggage. If Thuy Van
was working, she'd do the typing of the MTA;
if not, the other airman had me do it so I'd
learn how.

There were a lot of "freedom birds" arriving and departing Bien Hoa Air Base during
the last months of 1971. These were commercial contract airlines like Seaboard World,
Airlift International, Saturn, Trans International, Universal Airlines, World Airlines,
Braniff, etc. If my office had no in-country
flights to process, then I'd be called upon
to drive a warehouse tug pulling a set of
steps or staircases as they were also called,
that were mounted on a steel frame with
wheels. Two of them were positioned at each
aircraft; one at the front door and one at
the back. Arriving passengers would go out
both doors to empty out the plane quickly.
Departing passengers would go up both steps
for quick loading of the aircraft.

Anyone who ever served in Vietnam can

identify with this. Whenever I left the air
conditioned comfort of my Tri Service ATCO
office or the snack bar, it didn't take long
to start sweating. This part of the country
was hot and humid all year long. The main
area of the terminal at Bien Hoa where the
passengers sat, had ceiling fans mounted
high over their heads and a few stand-up
fans to help circulate the hot, humid air.
The fans helped, but only a little bit.

Out in the direct sunlight where the
planes parked, it was extremely hot and
humid so our goal was to get the passengers
on and off the aircraft quickly. Once the
engines of a plane were turned off, the
planes heated up real fast.

One day a passenger checked in with me
during a rare slow day. He was an Army
helicopter door gunner, returning to the
States to attend his grandmother's funeral.
Because she had raised him, he was given a
priority travel status on his travel orders
that was a higher priority than ordinary
leave. During our conversation he told me
the life expectancy of a helicopter door
gunner in his unit was only six days. He'd
beaten the odds.

He told me that he needed money for his
trip and offered to sell me his camera for
$25.00. It was the kind that had self-de-
veloping film. After each picture was
taken, the film was automatically ejected
from the camera and the picture would de-
velope as you held it in your hand in only
60 seconds. I used that camera a lot whenever film for it was available and not too
expensive. At the time I bought it, film
was only $2.15 for eight photos. After the
price went up to $4.15, I didn't use it as
much.

While many people who served in Vietnam

would say their weapon, helmet and flak
jacket were some of the most important
things to them, and for good reason, for me,
my mosquito net and fan were on my list in
addition to my helmet and flak jacket as
being important. One night in Vietnam was
all it took to convince anybody of the
necessity for one's survival against one of
man's worst enemies - the mosquito. The
flies and cockroaches were bad too but I was
never bitten by either of those pests. The
rats in this country were a problem too and
around our barracks were poisoned rat baits
so that we didn't have any rats inside of our
barracks.

The mosquitos in Vietnam took a liking to
red-blooded Americans and you could often
smell mosquito spray being used somewhere in
the barracks and also outside at night when a
truck with a big mechanical sprayer mounted
on the back would drive around the base fog-
ging large areas at a time.

My room was located at the end of a hall
and near an exit door. After a few minutes
of spraying by that truck, any surviving
mosquitos congregated by our door and screened windows, trying to get inside to escape
the spray.

Luckily for us, the BX kept lots of bug
sprays in stock. Every night before going to
bed, we'd spray our rooms and especially
around the screened area along the outer wall
and then we'd take a walk while we waited for
the air in our rooms to clear. Sometimes
we'd return to the room and do a "body count"
of all the dead mosquitos on the floor.

My favorite bug game was a little weird
now that I think about it but back then I
thought of it as being entertaining. Kids,
don't try this at home. It was played with
cockroaches, the bigger the better. To begin, a piece of food would be placed in the
middle of the cement floor, away from any-

thing that might burn. Everyone would sit
on a chair, keeping their feet off the floor
and trying to remain still. Once the cockroach crawled out of its hiding place and
busied itself on its meal, someone would
very quietly pour lighter fluid in a circle
around the cockroach. If there were two or
more of them, bets were made on which one
would last longer. If there was only one,
bets were made on how many seconds it would
last.

The circle of lighter fluid was then lit.
The floor was cement so we had no worries
about anything catching fire. Usually the
cockroaches would ignore the flames, continuing to eat the food. With the ring of fire
about a foot or more away from them, they
couldn't feel the heat. Then while the circle was still burning well, drops of lighter fluid were squirted onto the backs of the
cockroaches. After only a few seconds, the
fluid began to irritate the cockroaches
quite a bit.

This is when the excitement really began.
At this point, the cockroaches would be running around crazily as the lighter fluid began soaking into them and affecting their
nervous system. Sometimes both ugly brown
cockroaches would run through the circle of
fire and burst into flames at the same time,
like miniature cars with exploding gas
tanks. In this case, all bets were cancelled and the room was sprayed with a room de-
oderizer to get rid of the smell of burned
lighter fluid and burned cockroaches, now
referred to as "crispy critters." If one
cockroach survived longer than the other
and a bet was won, the loser of the bet was
responsible for cleaning up the mess. Game
over. Weird, huh?

While some kids would go outside in the
summer months with a magnifying glass and
"zap" ants on the sidewalk using the rays of

the sun, this cockroach game of ours was along the same idea, just taken up a notch or two.

I checked my mailbox at the base post office every day after work. Getting a letter from home was important to me and they always cheered me up. I tried to answer each one. It was good getting letters from friends and other relatives too and I received a lot of mail each month. I stayed busy writing lots of letters in return.

November 5th was my first day off since getting here. I was told that I may work on the night shift starting sometime in December. Previously I'd been told that I'd change shifts soon. My supervisor left for his home on November 4th on his 30-day leave. There seemed to be a shortage of supervisors as another airman and I were left to run the office and both of us had only one stripe. A staff sergeant stopped by the office one day and told us that he was in charge of us until our supervisor returned. He stepped in to help out a few times when one of us was off duty and it got busy with some flights to process. Otherwise, he left us alone to handle things and we did that most of the time.

Just like stores back home, the BX started selling Christmas cards and holiday decorations the first part of November. I bought some cards and small blinking lights to put up around the room in the barracks. One of my roommates bought a small green metal tree. War or no war, we were determined to celebrate Christmas and give our room a holiday look.

I think one of my roommates may have invented the first stereo surround sound

system, at least the first one any of us had
ever seen. I had two speakers hooked up to
my stereo. He took the two from his system
and one that he'd just bought from another
guy and hooked the extra three speakers into
my stereo. He placed two of the speakers in
the bedroom and kept three in the livingroom.
We were surrounded by sound!

He was good at other types of electrical
work too so he wired a lightbulb socket onto
one of the overhead beams in the bedroom so
we could have some light in there. When we
first built our rooms, none of them had overhead light fixtures. There were no light
switches either. To turn the light on and
off, you had to stand on a chair and screw
the lightbulb into the fixture to have light
and unscrew it with your hand to turn the
light off. Primitive, but effective. Some
of the other rooms in this barracks had a
similar situation with lighting.

Armed Forces Network broadcast news on the
radio and they had a TV station in Saigon as
well. We got pretty good reception of their
radio and TV channels since we were no more
than 20 or so miles from their broadcast
tower. Their TV station showed mostly old
movies and re-runs of TV shows and up-to-date
news.

We also got news from the Pacific Stars
and Stripes newspaper that was printed in
Japan and flown to Vietnam daily. The big
news story on November 7, 1971 was about a
visit by Secretary of Defense Melvin Laird.
He met with press agents at a news conference
at Tan Son Nhut Air Base in Saigon. General
Creighton Abrams and Ambassador Ellsworth
Bunker met with him there too.

When I wrote to my parents that week, I
told them about the special detail that I had
to work on during the afternoon of November

6th. It was just one of many details I'd be
on over the next year. Several of us had to
clear everything out of the upper floor rooms
of a neighboring barracks so it could be
boarded up. They figured it was safer with
nobody living on the 2nd floor if a mortar or
rocket hit the building.

While I was working on that detail, two
friends of mine went to Saigon. They told me
about their trip right after they got back.
One of them said it was bigger than Dallas,
Texas. That's pretty big! He said people
drove all over the road, left or right side
with no care for speed limits, lights or stop
signs. He said they got scared just riding
in a taxi.

At 5:30 p.m. a siren went off on base every
day. To me it meant chow time. Most of the
time we didn't have any flights to work that
time of the day. Then after work I headed
over to the post office. That week I'd
written to my Grandma Crews, Grandma and
Grandpa Smith, Aunt Francis and Uncle Jack
and friends I'd known in college. That was a
personal record for me to have written so
many letters in such a short period of time.

One of my roommates bought a miniature
Christmas tree that was very small, but we
had no place to put it. Our rooms were small
and with the furniture we had, there just
wasn't any space left. He made a shelf for
it on the wall opposite from the front door
of the livingroom at eyeball level. We also
put up a big sign that was bought in the BX.
It said, "Merry Christmas and Happy New Year"
and was placed over the top of the Christmas
tree shelf. When we received Christmas cards
in the mail, we put them on the wall around
the small shelf with the tree on it. It just
wouldn't be Christmas without a tree, even a
tiny one, so we made the best of it with what

we had.

I put my string of tiny blinking Christmas tree lights up around the perimeter of
the ceiling since I had no tree to put them
on. I had another string of them and put
them around the frame of my lower bunk,
along the legs of the bed and across the
lower bed springs of the top bunk in such a
way that my bed was now framed in tiny
blinking Christmas tree lights.

I got a kick out of it because it made
for a great conversation piece and it was
unique, to say the least. When I turned on
the lights and showed it to our Mama-san for
the first time, she said, "You beau coup
dinkai dau GI" which means, you are a very
crazy GI! A lot of jokes were made about my
bed by my friends and roommates. Well, I
thought, I'm in a crazy place to begin with,
dealing with a crazy military-political situation, living with other crazy people, so
why not? I removed the lights right after
Christmas.

I had to take my fatigue shirts that I'd
been issued in basic training to a tailor
shop and made into short sleeve shirts. They
only issued long sleeves when I went through
basic training in the summer of 1971. Bien
Hoa was just too hot and humid year round for
those. It was awhile before I got any
jungle fatigues.

One day I went to the barber shop close to
the Consolidated Open Mess for a trim. I
thought it would be just like any other
barber shop on a military base but this one
was very different. In addition to the male
barbers, there were female employees too.
For a fee, you could get a manicure, pedi-
cure, or face massage. The neck rub and
shoulder massage was given free after the
hair cut by the male barbers. I'd never

experienced anything like it. I felt un-
comfortable during the neck rub and shoulder
massage. I always cut my own nails and
couldn't imagine letting someone else do it
for me, even though it wasn't expensive.
When the barber used a straight razor on my
lower neck and around my ears, I kept thinking to myself, what if this guy is a Viet
Cong and decided to slit my throat? Sometimes I worried too much.

When the Mama-sans who worked in our barracks took a lunch break, they would gather
together in the hallway and squat down to
eat. They put plates of dried fish, rice and
some type of green vegetables or a soup on
the cement floor. They could have used the
card table in our break room across from our
room but they never did. They used a
fermented fish sauce on their food called
nuoc mam. It came in bottles about the size
of a wine bottle and smelled like rotten fish
to me. It really stunk up the place. Their
breath smelled like it too, a very strong
odor.
All of the mama-sans dressed the same way
whether they were young or old. They wore
rubber-soled sandals that looked like they
were made from old tire treads. We called
them Ho Chi Minh sandals. When outdoors,
they wore conical hats made of woven straw.
They were tied to their heads with strips of
cloth that was knotted under their chins.
Their pants were always black, loose-looking
and reminded me of silk pajamas. No matter
how hot it was, they wore long sleeved shirts
that were either white or pale yellow.
Their shirts were also made of a very light-
weight material and were also loose fitting.
Most of the mama-sans could speak a few
words of English. They probably knew more of
our language than we did of theirs. They had
passes to get on base. They wore them on a

string around their necks. Somehow, they always knew if the base was going to be attacked. We knew that because none of them showed
up for work until the day after. How they
found out, I'll never know. Only a few Vietnamese civilians worked on base at night and
most of them worked at the clubs.

On garbage collection day, Vietnamese men
wearing western-style clothes drove a very
large truck up to each dumpster. Their pri-
vately-owned truck was as big as an Army
deuce-and-a-half. It had wooden sides and
tailgate and had an aluminum cover over the
cargo area. The dumpsters didn't have tops
on them and to empty them, the men had to
climb into them and remove everything by
hand.

When the garbage men found anything they
could sell, like cardboard or soft drink cans
or glass bottles, they'd seperate that stuff
from the rest of the trash. There were Vietnamese houses near Long Binh Army Base made
almost entirely out of flattened-out soft
drink cans. Old tires were turned into sandals and they could find a use for most of
the stuff that GIs threw away.

One thing we badly needed for our room
but couldn't get for awhile was paint. Half
of our walls were plain, unpainted, brown
plywood. The other half was light blue, but
not evenly distributed.

I traveled from Charleston Air Force Base
in South Carolina to West Georgia College in
Carrollton, Georgia in September 1969. My
bus stopped in Atlanta and I bought a large
Confederate battle flag at the gift shop in
the bus station. I hung it on a wall of my
dorm room while I was a student at WGC. I
left the flag at my parent's house when I enlisted in the Air Force in June 1971. When I
got to Vietnam, they mailed it to me and I
put it to good use covering up a large sect-

ion of a wall that was unpainted.

I found some posters while on a room
cleaning-out detail and put those on the
walls too. One of them had a drawing of an
Army soldier wearing a helmet, backpack, and
carrying an M-16 rifle. The words printed on
the poster were: "Visit facinating Vietnam,
fun capital of the world." A slightly smaller poster I'd found had a drawing of a B-52
bomber flying over a jungle scene with the
words, "This vacation visit beautiful Vietnam." I also found a large colorful poster
with the words "Butterfly of Love" printed
over a large colorful butterfly. One of my
favorite posters was one of the singer James
Taylor. Big eyes were taped over the original ones so that he had a weird spaced-out
look. I also had a poster of the lead singer
of the band, Herman's Hermits. What we lack-
ed in paint for color, we made up for in
colorful posters.

On November 10th, the other airman in my
office was dismissed from working in Tri-
Service ATCO for goofing off. He had been my
trainer while A1C Davis was on leave. That
left just Thuy Van and I to run things.
Davis wasn't due back for another three
weeks. I was supposed to be off the next day
but now had to work and teach a new guy who
was being temporarily assigned here how to do
the work that I just finished learning how to
do myself. We were short of people and that
was just the way things were.

Even though I missed out on getting a day
off that week, at least I didn't have to work
more than my normal 12-hour shift. That
night I went to the movie theater and saw
Kelly's Heroes. The base theater was really
nice. I enjoyed the hot buttered popcorn and
the cool dry air from the huge air conditioner the building had.

There was fighting going on in other loca-

tions throughout Vietnam at the time. Just
not here. I knew my parents would see film
footage of some of that fighting on the
evening news almost every night. That's why
I tried to stress to them in my letters that
it wasn't happening here and that I was just
fine.

Sometimes it seemed like the days were
just a carbon copy of the previous day. Get
up, get dressed, walk to the chow hall for
breakfast, walk to work. Get off work, walk
to the post office, walk to the barracks then
to the chow hall for supper, then walk back
to the barracks again. I got plenty of ex-
ercise walking.

Our detachment didn't have to run the
annual mile-and-a-half run that we'd been
told in basic training was an annual requirement. I don't know why we didn't have
to, I was just glad that we didn't.

My facial hair grew so slowly then that I
could go several days without shaving. The
hair on my head grew slowly too. It was
still so short from the basic training cut
that it still wasn't long enough to comb. I
only needed a trim around my ears and the
back of my neck, nothing off the top or
sides.

I didn't drink coffee then and the milk in
the chow hall wasn't real, tasting like powdered milk to me. That's why I drank either
some kind of juice if available or some type
of drink that tasted like a fruit punch-
flavored drink. Sometimes for breakfast I'd
have an omelet or pancakes with sausage.
When my lunch break came around, if it was
real busy or if it was raining, I'd eat a
couple of chili dogs with some french fries
at the snack bar close to the terminal.
Every once in a while, somebody was able to
borrow the OIC's blue half-ton pickup truck
and take a bunch of us to the chow hall and
back. At the time, Captain Love was the OIC

(Officer-In-Charge) of the passenger terminal.

   I'd never been in a place where it rained
so hard. I remember walking one day with my
poncho on and the rain was coming down so
hard that I had trouble breathing. I had to
use my right hand to constantly wipe my face
like a windshield wiper going full speed to
be able to see where I was going and to keep
from drowning while walking. It felt like I
was walking through a waterfall, it was raining so hard. No wonder our base had big
cement-lined drainage ditches all over it.
Without those, we'd probably be under water
or washed away. There were only two seasons
here instead of the four we were used to back
home. Here it was either hot and dry or hot
and wet. I arrived during the rainy season
and it certainly was living up to its name.
   When I took my poncho off, I was soaking
wet. It protected me from the rain, but not
the heat and humidity. I was soaked from my
own sweat. That's why some guys I knew
didn't even bother putting on a poncho when
it was raining. They knew they'd just end up
all wet anyway. At least wearing my poncho
helped keep my mail dry when I went to the
post office and found letters in my mail box.

   Some of my friends had never been away
from home before, at least so far away and
for so long. It took some getting used to.
We used to talk about how to deal with it
sometimes. I tried to develop a mind-set,
"home is where you sleep." Some people
found some relief by drinking, others by doing drugs. I turned to music and hanging out
with my friends, who became sort of like a
family in a way.

   Photography was my new hobby since I'd
gotten an easy to use camera. Whenever I got

a day off I'd go around taking pictures of
just about everything: where I worked, where
I lived, people I knew, rainbows, wooden
benches that had words printed on them, air-
planes, lizards, helicopters, buildings, etc.
I eventually ended up with two photo albums
full of pictures. A lot more were sent back
to the States to friends and family.

I took my camera to work with me some
days. I tried to get a picture of every airline company plane that had a contract with
the government flying troops into and out of
Bien Hoa Air Base. There were planes in and
out of here almost every day so I had many
opportunities.

My second hobby was reading, even though I
didn't have much time for it. I had a few
paperbacks with my favorite ones being full
of Charlie Brown cartoons by Charles Schultz.

One day at work I met an Australian nurse.
She told me some interesting stories about
her four years in Vietnam. She said that
she'd only spent 56 days at home during all
that time. I wish that I'd either had my
tape recorder with me or some paper to write
on because she told me some terrible stories
about stuff she'd seen in Vietnam. She said
the My Lai massacre was nothing compared to
what the Viet Cong did to people.

Thuy Van had been a nurse and field inter-
preter for two years before she started working in the Tri-Service ATCO office. She also
told me many interesting stories. At the
time I thought to myself, maybe I'll write a
book about these women's stories when I get
home. Now I can't remember their stories at
all.

One subject that was discussed a lot during November was whether or not we'd be in
Vietnam long enough to get credit for this
tour of duty. I remember someone saying that

we had to be here for six full months to get
credit. Tens of thousands of Americans were
leaving Vietnam each month as part of the
Vietnamization program.

There were rumors going around that we all
might be leaving early next year. Every time
a story appeared in the Pacific Stars and
Stripes newspaper about the troop pull-outs
from Vietnam, speculation about our futures
became a major topic of discussion. That
made it harder to be positive about our reason for being here in the first place. As
Americans accustomed to winning wars, it
didn't seem like we were winning anything
here. And what about all those 50,000 Americans who already died in Vietnam and the
likelyhood that more would die? What did
they die for? What did we accomplish other
than delay the Communist takeover? Most of
us didn't have much faith in the ability of
the South Vietnamese to win this war by
themselves.

The South Koreans, Australians and everyone else who sent any troops here had either
already left or were, like us, just about
gone. By the end of 1971, only one div-
ision-size U.S. ground combat unit remained
in Vietnam. By the middle of March 1972, the
101st Airborne Division stationed at Phu Bai
was gone. They were the last big unit to go.

Imagine yourself being the back-up
quarterback on a football team. It's the
last game of the season and you've been sitting on the bench watching from the sidelines
all season long, not having gotten the chance
to play even one set of downs in any of the
games. In this final game, it's the fourth
quarter and your team is down 45-0. Many of
your teammates have been knocked out of the
game due to injuries and now your coach sends
you and a few others into the game with only
a few minutes left on the game clock. You
know that no matter how well you play, you

can't possibly win the game. The fact is,
your chances of getting hurt like so many
others have, is far greater than your
chances of winning, especially because your
best defensive and offensive players are no
longer in the game. To make matters even
worse, the crowds in the stands, who initially cheered for your team when they first
ran onto the field, are now booing loudly and
some are even spitting at you and throwing
objects onto the field.

That's the way I felt at this time in my
life. American troops had been killed and
wounded since the early 1960s and now instead of over 500,000 of us in Vietnam with a
chance of winning the war, there are only 10%
of that number left and we're only getting a
few replacements. For my unit, I was one of
the very last replacements it ever got.

Someone asked this question one day, "Who
wants to be the last American to die in Vietnam for a lost cause?" Not me! In my opinion, the low morale of troops within U.S.
military units in Vietnam at this time was
due to our politicians who put us in the game
with no plan to win, no will to win, and
worse still, put so many restrictions on how
we were to conduct this war that it made it
easier for the enemy to eventually win and
made it impossible for us and the South Vietnamese and its other allies to win.

Around the middle of November 1971, a few
of the guys on this hall in my barracks decided to clean up one of the empty rooms to
use it as a card-playing room. All of the
rooms we slept in were too small for four
people to play cards in so now we'd have a
place for that. Playing cards was a good way
to relax after a long day and socialize with
our friends. We played mostly games called
Hearts or Spades. With few exceptions, we
didn't play for money, just for fun. I lost

500 pennies in an all night game of penny
ante blackjack once. I learned my lesson and
that lesson was that I wasn't a very good
card player. At least it was only pennies
and not dollars.

Around that time our favorite newspaper
published an article about 45,000 more U.S.
troops that would leave Vietnam by the first
of February 1972. I sure hoped so. After
all the troops were gone then we'd find out
whether or not we'd wasted ten years and
over 50,000 lives.

I went to the BX one day in November to
buy some color film for my camera. I was
shocked at the new price it was now being
sold for. I had bought some for $2.15 not
long ago and now the price was $4.15! I
couldn't understand how that could have
happened because I'd heard that Congress
put a price freeze on stuff because of inflation.

One evening while I was standing in line
at the movie theater, I noticed a steel and
concrete structure nearby. It reminded me
of the type of machine gun pillbox you might
see on the Normandy beaches of France back in
1944. There were narrow slits on some of its
irregular-shaped sides for the occupants to
shoot their weapons from. There was a round
steel dome at the top, raised above the concrete structure in a way that would allow
someone to look out all around it from all
sides and shoot weapons out in all directions
as well.

I was told that the French built it when
they built this base a long time ago. Because it was so big and solid, American
forces had to build around it when they took
over this part of the base. There was no way
it could be gotten rid of without damaging
other buildings nearby.

Another thing the French left from their war in Vietnam was an old fighter plane. It was built in America during World War II and was called a "Bearcat." It was mounted on a pedestal in front of the Vietnamese base headquarters building.

It seemed like it was hot here every day but we actually did get a cool spell every once in a while. These times were few and far between so they were easy to forget that they ever happened. Slow days at work were like that too. Every once in a while we'd get one, but so few that they were easily forgotten as well. Whenever I had a slow day at work, I took advantage of the time and wrote letters home or to friends and other relatives.

Thuy Van, the Vietnamese secretary, came in late one morning because the MPs at the gate gave her a hard time. She had a pass but the MP told her she needed an Air Force pass. That was not true. The other secretaries in our unit didn't need or have any other type of pass. The MPs just picked on her for no reason. They were just a bunch of smart-alecks looking for trouble. Thuy Van came in very mad and told the Captain. It was enough to make anybody mad. Guys like those MPs didn't help the Army make a good impression on the Vietnamese.

On November 17th I went to the movie theater and saw a war movie, Mosquito Squadron. A day or two after that I was able to get some white paint and started painting our walls in the barracks. The white paint made the rooms look bigger, brighter, and the walls were all the same color for the first time.

Some days we'd hear or read about an attack at another base and wonder when we'd

get hit. We all agreed that it was just a
matter of time. Sometimes we'd discuss what
we'd do in the event we did get attacked and
how we'd try to find a safe place to take
cover. Our shelters were falling apart,
boarded up, and couldn't be used.

One day when I was walking from the post
office to my barracks, a small light tan-
colored puppy walked up to me. I didn't see
it until it was right at my feet because I
was reading a letter as I walked. I stopped
and looked around to see if anyone was looking for it. When it followed me all the way
to my room, I decided to keep the dog and
named him Sandy because of the color of his
fur. He wasn't around for more than a few
days. He just wandered off one day and I
never saw him again. One of my friends suggested that he became the supper of some
Vietnamese since it was known that they ate
dogs. I hoped not. He was a cute and
friendly pup.

On November 18th I had to work until 9
and I was just too tired to do anything but
sleep when I got back to the barracks. The
plane was two hours behind schedule and we
had twenty five people on emergency leave to
put on it. That was an unusual flight to
process.
November 19th was my day off and I'd
planned to see the movie Love Story. Thuy
Van went to Tan Son Nhut Air Base and saw it
and she said it was really good so I was going to find out for myself. The line was so
long that evening that I gave up and went
back to my barracks.

Around this time a lot of guys were getting out of Passenger Service, cross training into other career fields for various
reasons. I was told that there was no

demand for this career field in the U.S. and
in order for me to keep from having to cross
train into something else, I'd have to
either extend here or volunteer for overseas
duty elsewhere. Those people who didn't
cross train voluntarily would get assigned as
a cook or security police at their next
assignment in the U.S. I talked to the First
Sergeant and the Detachment Commander about
that and they both suggested I cross train.
I didn't want to go through any more training
after I'd gone through this much, especially
not when I was just getting used to the job
here and liked it. I decided I'd rather put
in for overseas or extend than cross train.

My first supervisor was coming back for
his second tour on December 5th and he said
he was returning for the same reason. So I
figured I could make more money here, spend
less here (all tax-free), stay single here
and be able to come out of the Air Force with
experience in this career field which could
help me get a job with a civilian airlines
after returning home. I had no military
career aspirations then. I'd do my four
years and then go back to civilian life.

There had been lots of people extending
here. One of my tech school instructors was
at Bien Hoa for three years and he said he
wanted to come back again because of the extra pay. The new pay raise would go into
effect soon and that's one more reason to extend. I thought that if I put my money in
the 10% savings plan, I could make a lot more
money than I could in the U.S. Of course the
main drawback would be being away from home
for so long. At the time, I thought that
everyone had to break away from home sometime
and the time for me seemed like now.

The third week of November we had a few
days of unusually cool weather. Thuy Van
told me that it was the beginning of the Viet-

namese winter. It got down to 58 degrees at
night, which was a lot cooler than it had
been. It was a welcome relief from the heat
and humidity we'd been experiencing up to now.
Even after a cool night, it still got up into
the 80s in the afternoon.

After thinking about it for awhile, I
finally went to CBPO and filled out a form we
called a "dream sheet," where you listed in
order the places you dreamed about being sent
to next. I put in for "world wide" for overseas choices and Charleston Air Force Base as
my first stateside choice. World wide for an
overseas choice meant that I'd accept an
assignment anywhere in the world outside of
the United States.

Money was an incentive for many of the
choices made by military personnel since we
didn't get paid very much in 1971. Back then
most GIs qualified for food stamps because of
their low income. Since I'd enlisted in
Georgia, the state took some of my pay for
state income tax. The federal government
took some for income tax too and social security and I was in Vietnam my second month
before they quit taxing me. When you worked
twelve hours a day for six or more days in a
row and you knew that the guys stationed back
in the States were working eight hours a day
and only five days in a row, you felt like
you were making less than minimum wage.

While stationed in Vietnam, the good thing
about pay was, no taxes were taken out of my
paycheck after November and I received hostile
fire pay, which some called "combat pay."
That was an extra $55.00 a month. Also,
things like hair cuts, clothing upkeep and
stuff like that cost less here than back in
the U.S. so I was left with more money each
month.

If I'd been in the Army or Marine Corps and
had to fight in the jungles of Vietnam and

live in the mud in a hole in the ground, no
amount of extra money would have influenced
me to stay even one day longer than I had to.
However, being stationed on an air base with
Army troops and helicopter gunships nearby
and not being attacked so far made the extra
money seem like a good deal in exchange for
staying here possibly even beyond my one
year tour. I'm sure there were some guys in
the Army and Marine Corps who would have
gladly traded places with me if given the
opportunity. Also, at the time, I was living with a false sense of security. This
base wasn't as safe and secure as I thought
it was. As I would soon find out, in Vietnam, things could change a lot in the blink
of an eye. I had much to learn.

I talked to some guys who had been either
stationed in Thailand or had been there on
R & R. They said it was a good place to be
if you wanted to stay in Asia. I went to
CBPO again and talked to a guy who worked in
the enlisted assignments section to see if I
could get stationed there next. He told me
there were no openings for my AFSC (career
field) but that by putting in for "World-
wide" I had a good chance of staying somewhere in Asia, just not there. I'd already
done that so I was back to square one. An
Air Force AFSC was similar to an Army MOS in
that it was a specialty code associated with
a particular type of job.

One of my concerns at this time was to be
awarded my 5-skill level so I could get promoted. To do that, I had to read several
volumns of books about my career field. Our
unit training manager ordered them for me
and when they arrived, he briefed me on what
I had to do. For each book, I had to take
an open-book test and he'd review the results with me. Then, when he felt I was

ready, he'd order the closed-book test for me.
I had to pass that before he'd order the next
one. With all that additional reading and
studying to do and still work a 12-hour shift,
that left me less time each day for anything
else. I really felt the pressure to score
well on the tests. I don't remember my
scores but I know that I passed each test and
that's what counted most to me. The books
arrived on November 23rd and the course had to
be done by December 23rd.

I'd already planned on going to the movies
on November 24th to see Valdez Is Coming, so I
put off reading any of my CDCs (Career Devel-
opment Course) until the next day.

That week I received my first issue of
jungle fatigues. I'd already been here a full
month. I was given four shirts but only one
pair of pants to go with them. Supply was out
of my size. I had to take the shirts to get
tailored. It only cost me $6.50 to have the
sleeves cut short and hemmed, the sides taken
in and the bottom cut off some. They also
sewed on my stripes and name tag. The shirts
I was given originally looked like they could
have fit a giant instead of me, so they were
altered quite a bit. The pants I got didn't
come from Supply. A friend of mine who was at
Long Binh Army Base got me a pair of slightly
faded Army jungle fatigue pants. I had to get
them tailored too because they were too long
and too baggy.

We had our second drug briefing on November
24th. It seemed like the Army was having most
of the problems since I'd gotten here. An
Army enlisted man at their base across the
other side of the flightline from us died the
other day from a heroin overdose. The Air
Force had its share of drug problems too, I
just didn't know how bad at this time. A
friend of mine who worked at that base said

when the guy's roommate found him, his hands were turning blue and there were needle marks on his arm. By the time he got to the hospital (dispensary), he was blue all over, and very dead. You could get a vile of 90% pure heroin for only $5.00 here so that was a big part of the problem, that it was cheap and plentiful. In the U.S., the same amount of heroin sold for $25.00 and it was only about 15% pure. That's why it was so tempting for some people.

At that time I had no idea that Bien Hoa Air Base was about to be attacked and that my life and those of my friends and co-workers there would be changed forever. A peaceful chapter of my life was about to end. The reality of the war in Vietnam, that had so far seemed far away, was about to give us a wake-up call. We were about to start a new chapter of our lives.

The Viet Cong had been attacking Bien Hoa Air Base since the early 1960s. They used mortars and rockets fired from a distance most of the time. Every once in a while they'd sneak onto the base by crawling under barbed wire and through mined areas with the explosives they carried on themselves. During the 1968 Tet Offensive, they conducted a large ground attack and tried to overrun the base.

They had some of their people working on base as day laborers and knew where all of our facilities, planes and helicopters were located. It was never a matter of IF they would attack again. They kept us in suspense as to WHEN and HOW. They also knew about American holidays and when most GIs would be off duty, like on weekends also. The Viet Cong were cunning and patient.

November 25, 1971 was Thanksgiving, a traditional American holiday. Around 2:45 a.m., I was awakened by a loud noise. A

second or two later there were a couple of
more loud noises and I scrambled out of bed as
fast as I could. I would have been under my
bed faster had I not gotten tangled up in the
mosquito net, almost ripping it apart on my
way to the floor. We'd been instructed to
take cover under our beds if we were in the
barracks during an attack. Since we had no
other shelter for protection from bullets or
bomb blasts, our helmets, flak jackets and
beds would have to do.

Shortly after the third explosion and
after I was on the cement floor, the base
siren went off, warning us that we were under attack. As if three loud explosions
weren't enough of a clue as to what was
happening, now we had to listen to a super
loud siren that sounded like the tornado
warning sirens used in some communities back
in the States. I was bothered more by the
annoying sound of the siren than I was the
three explosions that woke me up. At least
they produced only a short-duration noise.
Finally the siren stopped and all was eerily
quiet again. After a short discussion between my two roommates and I, we went back to
sleep again, but only after we were convinced that we weren't about to be overrun by
attacking hordes of Viet Cong.

One of my friends and I borrowed a warehouse tug from work the next day and set out
to find where the morter rounds or rockets
had hit. I had my camera with me and we asked around until we got the information we
needed to go right to the locations. The
first stop was an aircraft revetment near the
flightline. These things were made of two
walls of metal with sand packed in between.
We could easily see the damage near the top
of one of the revetments. It didn't seem
like a lot of damage so we figured it may
have been hit by a small mortar, maybe a 60mm
in size. I got a couple of pieces of

shrapnel for souvineers.

The second location we drove to was a
fenced-in parking lot and storage area.
There was a big hole in the asphalt-paved
lot not too far from the surrounding fence.
I took a picture of it through the chain-
linked fence. A guy we talked to there said
there had been a 40-foot long flatbed trailer parked over the hole. The trailer was
loaded with huge spools of telephone cable.
The mortar or rocket had gone through the
spool of cable and the trailer and exploded
in the ground under it, blowing the trailer
into small pieces. Those pieces had already
been cleaned up by the time we got there.

I don't remember whose idea it was to
climb over the fence and take a close-up
picture of the hole but my friend and I did
just that. The hole was big enough to put
both of my feet in it. That's when I noticed a metal object, which I figured to be a
part of the mortar or rocket. I reached
down into the bottom of the hole and tried
to pull it out, right after I took a picture
of it. I told my friend that if I could get
it out, it would be a neat souvineer to
have.

Just then a blue pickup truck with the
letters "EOD" painted on the door pulled up
near us. EOD stands for Explosive Ordinance
Disposal. The driver asked us what we were
doing and I told him about my plan. He told
us to get away from there because there
might be an unexploded warhead buried at the
far end of the metal object I just pulled on
and it could explode at any time. I hadn't
even thought about that, nor had my friend.
We cleared out of there quick! I thanked
the guy from EOD and counted my blessings.
I got a great picture of the object in the
hole and lived to tell about it. We were
not able to find where the third mortar or
rocket had hit. I learned a valuable

lesson that day. Look, but don't touch! If
you're not sure about something when it comes
to explosive devices, call EOD.

We later learned that our first attack
since our arrival had resulted in no casualties. Well, no human casualties anyway. A 7-
inch long lizard was killed at the aircraft
revetment.

The last time Bien Hoa was attacked prior
to this was October 4, 1971 which was just a
few weeks prior to our arrival. While this
was only a small attack, it sent us a message.
The Viet Cong were in the area and could still
do some damage. It also caused us to make
sure our helmets and flak jackets were within
reach and that we had nothing stored under our
beds, which became our shelters during
attacks. My first experience of being on the
receiving end of an attack also gave me something else to write home about. Things like
this might make the nightly news back home so
I had to reassure my parents that I was still
OK. I didn't dare tell my parents how stupid
I'd been in trying to pull out the metal object from that hole in the ground which might
have blown up in my face. Some things didn't
make it into my letters and that was one of
those things.

I had to work Thanksgiving Day. I wasn't
alone when it came to working. The cooks in
the Bien Hoa Air Base chow hall really put in
some long hours of hard work to give us a
great Thanksgiving feast. Everything you'd
expect in a big buffet-style restaurant in the
States this holiday was served to us and it
was just fantastic. MREs (Meals Ready to Eat)
hadn't been invented yet so back then if you
didn't get a hot meal in a chow hall or one
delivered by helicopter from a field kitchen,
your meal came in a little green can. Canned
food beats no food at all, but nothing beats a
good hot meal prepared in a chow hall, consid-

ering the options.

While sitting around eating or meeting
other GIs for the first time in other situations, one of the first topics discussed
was home. Everyone wanted to know where you
were from. Some GIs even had the name of
their home state sewn onto their boonie hats.
These were wide-brimmed, dark green hats with
a dark green string that hung down from both
sides so you could tighten the hat down on
your head to keep it from blowing away or to
hold your hat on your back if you took it off
when indoors and it was held to your body by
the string. Black thread was the color used
to form the letters of the states sewn onto
the hats.

Some of the guys on our hall in the barracks made a change one day to the room across
from ours that had been made into a card
playing room. Somebody put a TV on a stand
in there and enough chairs to seat about 20
people. Now we could play cards and watch TV
at the same time. It turned out real nice
and my roommates and I went there to hang out
with our friends.

One day at work, I checked my mail during
my lunch break. I got a package from home
and opened it up as soon as I got back to the
office. Thuy Van saw me taking out all kinds
of stuff like candy and pre-sweetened powdered drinks from the package. She went to some
of the other offices to get some of her Vietnamese friends to come and see what my parents had sent. I called this a "care package." When the Vietnamese women saw all the
stuff I'd gotten from home, they laughed and
called me "Baby-san" because to them, grown
men didn't get candy and other goodies from
their mothers, only babies did. They thought
that I was too old (I was 20 at the time) to
get this kind of stuff from my mother. After

they went back to their offices, I took some
of my candy to other offices around the terminal where some of my friends worked and
shared my stuff with them. Thuy Van and her
friends didn't get a thing.

CHAPTER THREE

DECEMBER 1971

Because I worked in the passenger terminal and had full access to the aircraft arrival and departure schedules, I was able to find out when all types of planes would be here. I was able to get a picture of a group of people coming off an old C-54 aircraft that had been built back in the 1940s. It was used by the Secretary of the Air Force and the group I saw was him and some of the officers traveling with him and the officers who met him when he got off the plane. My camera didn't have a zoom lens so everything appeared to be further away than it actually was.

The closer we got to Christmas, the more Christmas cards my roommates and I received. We put them all up on our livingroom wall and we almost ran out of wall space because we had so many. Had we not been in Vietnam, we probably wouldn't have received as many as we did. We even got some from church groups and people we normally wouldn't have heard from had we been at a stateside base. It was nice to know that so many other people were thinking about us now. It was such a morale booster to get all those cards.

We all agreed that none of us had ever spent a Christmas in such a hot and humid place. Even though we got a cool spell at night recently, compared to our respective states of Maine, Ohio and Georgia, this was really hot for December and for a holiday period when you're used to having much cooler weather.

On December 2nd I had to work from 7 a.m. until 4 a.m. December 3rd because of a very

busy flight schedule and some aircraft delays
of one type or another. We were short of
people so I had to be right back at work
again at 7 AM December 3rd with only a couple
of hours of sleep. At least the next shift
was only a regular 12-hour one. Then on December 4th I had to work from 7a.m. - 9:30p.m.,
a 14½-hour stretch. When I got back to the
barracks that night, I was beat. Later I
found out that some people from our detachment were sent TDY (temporary duty) somewhere
for awhile and that left us short-handed yet
again.

"Man must make an end to war or war will
make an end to man." I don't remember where I
found the quote by President John F. Kennedy
that I put in a letter home that first week in
December. I found it a bit ironic though because President Kennedy was responsible for
sending military advisors and millions of
dollars in foreign aid to South Vietnam in
support of their war against Communist insur-
gents. He supplied them with weapons, including aircraft of all types, boats, munitions and began our involvement in a war that
would eventually cost over 58,000 American
lives, hundreds of thousands wounded and
sharply divided our country.
When Richard Nixon ran for president, he
told the American public that his goal was to
achieve "peace with honor" in Vietnam. When
I watched helicopters land on the roof of the
American embassy in Saigon in April 1975 on
TV, taking out the last American and Vietnamese civilian employees in the final evacu-
ation, that didn't look like peace with honor
to me. I was in Vietnam when he was my Commander-In-Chief and I believed him.

A1C Davis returned from leave around December 5th. He was in charge of my office
when I arrived in October. With him back,

the work load eased up some. No sooner than
I thought that things might get a little
easier, he told me that he might go on night
shift to take charge and my old trainee who
was then on night shift, would come back to
day shift. Davis also said that everyone he
talked to said I was doing a good job and I
was going to be in charge of day shift for
good. That made me feel good to have only
one stripe and be in charge.

December 9th was a night to remember. It
was Armand Fecteau's birthday and he wanted
to throw a big party. We'd gone through tech
school together and after some room altera-
tions, he'd become one of my two roommates.
I don't know how many rum and colas I had but
they told me the next day that sometime during the party, I stood up on a chair and gave
some funny speeches. I really don't remember
that at all but I do remember a lot of people
stopping by to wish Armand a happy birthday
and everyone was drinking and joining in on
the celebration. That's another thing that
didn't make it into any of my letters home.

The base commander (a full-bird colonel),
inspected our barracks sometime during that
week in December. He said the halls and outside doors had to be painted white. I
thought our barracks would look like a ward
in a hospital if we did that, but of course
we had no choice.

There was another article in the newspaper
that week that the U.S. may pull out the last
of its troops from Vietnam by July 1, 1972.
I sure hoped so. Also that week, this time
on TV, we got a stateside weather report done
by a female. That was a first for me. All
my life I'd only seen men doing the weather
report on the news.
Another thing on TV that week was a foot-

ball game between the Minnesota Vikings and
the New Orleans Saints. I snacked a lot during the game. I'd weighed myself at work
earlier in the day on the baggage scales. I
weighed only 143 pounds, which is what I
weighed in 1968 when I played football during
my Senior year in high school. I could
afford to eat without worrying about being
overweight.

Long Binh Army Base was located between
Bien Hoa and Tan Son Nhut Air Base, which was
on the northwest side of Saigon. The two air
bases were only about 20 miles apart. Many
Army personnel would go to Long Binh after
arriving in-country. A lot of them would
process through the 90th Replacement Battalion (also known as the 90th Repo Depot).
There they would be given orders assigning
them to various units scattered around the
country. To get to those units, especially
those a long distance away, they'd either fly
from Tan Son Nhut or Bien Hoa.
   That's where one of my jobs came into play.
We had many U.S. Air Force C-130 Hercules
flights that carried troops and cargo from
Bien Hoa to different bases throughout the
country. My job was to announce the flights,
process the passengers and direct them to the
departure gate. If I had a chance, I'd take
a picture of them loading into their C-130 and
then their baggage pallet being loaded last.

Each month, Air Force personnel got a form
called a Leave And Earnings Statement. It had
a lot of different types of information on it,
most of it having to do with money. My base
pay for the period 1-30 November 1971 was
$234.10 and wasn't supposed to be taxed. The
Federal Government took out $14.08 for income
tax anyway. I didn't receive any pay or a
Leave And Earnings Statement for October 1971
so I don't know if they taxed my pay that

month or not. Back then things were a lot
cheaper so of course the pay was much lower
than it is now. I got $73.00 some months
and $74.00 other months extra for hostile
fire pay and foreign duty pay combined.

Sometime around the middle of December
there was talk about a Bob Hope USO show coming to the area, possibly at Long Binh Army
Base only a few miles from here. A friend
of mine and I asked our supervisor if we
could go. He wasn't sure if we could because if there was going to be a show there,
more aircraft than normal would land here
bringing in troops to see it. He told us
that since nobody else had asked, if anyone
was allowed to go, he would let the two of us
go but probably nobody else. That was alright with us. At least he didn't say no.
There was an Army shuttle bus that took
people from Bien Hoa to USARV (United States
Army, Republic of Vietnam) Headquarters at
Long Binh and MACV (Military Assistance Command, Vietnam) Headquarters in Saigon every
day. At least we'd have a way to get to the
show and back.

Bien Hoa Air Base got attacked for the
second time since I'd arrived here. On Friday night around midnight on December 17th,
I was sitting at the desk in my barracks
livingroom writing a letter. I heard some
distant "booms" and shortly afterwards the
base siren went off, warning of an attack. I
got under my bed as fast as I could. It was
the only safe place to be. When the siren
stopped, it became very quiet again. It
usually was very quiet this time of night.
At work the next day, I asked around to
find out if anyone knew where the mortars or
rockets hit and if there was any damage or
injuries. I wanted to take some pictures of
where the damage was done, if there was any.

The only person that was able to give me any
information was an Air Force security policeman. He came over to my office and put a fuse
on the counter to show me his souvineer. It
was real small, maybe three inches long. He
said it was from an 82mm mortar round that had
exploded last night on the Vietnamese side of
the base. He told me that a Vietnamese helicopter was damaged in the attack and nothing
else, as far as he knew. It was in a hanger
being repaired so I wouldn't be able to take
any pictures of it.

It rained real hard Sunday evening, December 19, 1971. For some reason, a friend of
mine decided to drink too much. I think it
was because he wasn't going to be able to
spend Christmas with his wife. That was pure
speculation on my part. He'd only gotten
married a short time before he joined the Air
Force. He said that he missed his wife a few
times that night. He was slurring his words a
lot and sometimes he'd say stuff that was
really funny and that's when I got out my
tape recorder and started recording it all. I
planned on letting him listen to himself the
next day after he'd sobered up. After awhile
though, he started yelling loudly and threat-
ened to kill some people and that got the
attention of some of the neighbors.
One of those neighbors was a big guy, very
muscular. He suggested that we take my friend
outside in the rain. He claimed that it
would help sober him up as well as any cold
shower would. At that time my friend was only
wearing his GI-issue white boxer shorts. The
problem was, he was so drunk that he couldn't
even stand up and was lying in his bed. He
continued to talk loudly and yelled out a
few times too. No problem! By this time
there were four or five guys in the room and
they lifted him up and carried him out to the
sidewalk which was only a few feet away.

While I took pictures, they laid him down in
the pouring rain. I stayed under the cover
of the steps that led up to the second floor
to keep my camera dry.

We were only out there for a couple of
minutes and then lightning struck overhead
and the thunder roared. We all said it at
the same time, "It's time to get back inside!" They carried him down the hall to a
shower stall and kept him in the cold
shower for a couple of minutes. Then they
took him back to his room and dried him off
and gave him some dry boxers to put on.

What happened next was so funny I just had
to take a picture of it. My friend put both
his legs into the same leg of his boxers and
then he couldn't figure out why they felt so
tight that he couldn't walk. It was hilari-
ous! He continued to say funny things and I
told him that if he didn't behave himself, I
was going to send his wife the tape recording
and pictures. That helped quiet him down a
little.

Another incident occurred just as we re-
entered his room from the shower. One of the
guys who'd helped carry him outside in the
rain had gotten wet too. He stood up on a
chair so he could screw in the lightbulb by
hand so we could have some light. There was
no lightswitch or pull-chain. He accidentally
touched the metal rim of the light socket and
the lightbulb at the same time as he was
screwing it in and yelled out a few choice
cuss words when he got the shock of his life.
Only a second before I'd told him to be care-
ful because he was all wet. Well, at least it
didn't kill him. It just gave him a jolt he'd
never forget!

And if that wasn't enough excitement for
one night, just as my friend was quieting
down in his bed and no longer threatening to
kill anybody, the base came under attack. We
were all talking about our drunk friend as my

tape recorder continued to record. We heard
some popping sounds coming from outside. Even
though it was raining real hard with loud
thunder and lightning, everyone heard those
distinct sounds and we just kind of looked at
one another until the base siren began blaring. Then everyone scattered, trying to find
a safe place to get to.

I'd been sitting on the floor next to a
bed with my tape player on it and I scooted
under it quickly. We knew what that siren
meant and reacted to it. Neither the attack
nor the siren lasted very long and after I
played the tape back, we could hear the
sounds of the popping noises, the base siren
and ourselves very clearly. To get an attack
on the base on tape was pure luck. To have
"dodged a bullet" again and live to tell
about it was even luckier still. After all,
these mortars and rockets that had been hitt-
ing the base could have killed or wounded
anyone near the impact area.

After the excitement of the attack died
down and the arguing about how many hits the
base took was stopped by the evidence played
out on the re-playing of my tape, my friends
went back to their rooms. The funniest thing
I'd seen in a long time was my drunk friend,
who slept through the loud base siren that
had blared out an attack warning and our loud
talking. I thought that nothing could wake
him up since all that noise didn't. I never
did send a copy of the tape recording or the
pictures to his wife. Lucky for him!

It continued to rain into the night.
Since it was still early, I decided to write
a letter home. I hadn't written home in a
while and now I had something exciting to
write about. It was my way of letting my
parents know that I was OK just in case the
attack made it on the evening news back home.

I found out the next day that 122mm rockets had hit the base, causing a lot of

damage to the American side of it. I went
around the base the next day and took some
pictures of the damage. I had the day off
so I had time to ask around and try to find
all of the places where the rockets hit. I
found out that there were a total of five
hits on this base and two rockets that hit
Tan Son Nhut Air Base.

A Special Services building was badly
damaged by one of the rockets and several
vehicles near it were destroyed. Nobody in
that building was hurt. Another of the
rockets hit beside a runway making a hole in
the ground and didn't cause any damage.
Another rocket hit only about twenty yards
from that one and went between a wall and a
roof and heavily damaged an F-5 Freedom
Fighter jet aircraft belonging to the VNAF
(Vietnamese Air Force), which I was able to
get a picture of. I couldn't find where two
of the rockets hit.

I got lucky on December 20th. In the BX
that day, I bought the last pack of color
film used by my camera that was in stock for
$2.15. The new shipment cost $4.15, so I
wouldn't be taking any more pictures with
this camera once I used up the film I had.

The reason I was able to get off on December 20th was because of what happened to
my friend. I talked to my supervisor the
night my friend got drunk and told him that
I felt like my friend needed someone to keep
an eye on him so if he threw up he wouldn't
choke to death on his own vomit. I was concerned about him and my supervisor respected
that and agreed that he shouldn't be left
alone in his condition. My supervisor actually stopped by to see for himself the condition that he was in and one of my roommates
told him about our efforts to sober him up
and eventually got him into some clean

clothes and put him to bed. I got someone to
take my place keeping an eye on him before I
left to take some pictures of the damage done
by the rocket attack.

After work on Friday December 24, 1971, a
friend of mine plus one of my roommates and I
got a pass to travel from Bien Hoa to Long
Binh. There was an outdoor ampitheater there
and that was where the USO-sponsored Bob Hope
Christmas Special was going to be on the 25th.
We took the regularly scheduled Army
shuttle bus over to Long Binh and then found
the barracks where one of our friends lived.
We spent the night there. I'll never forget
the latrine we had to use during our visit.
Instead of bathrooms with flush toilets like
we had at Bien Hoa in each barracks, the
troops here had to use a centrally-located 8-
hole outhouse. There was a stand-up fan at
one end to keep the air circulating inside of
the un-air conditioned building. There were
no stalls or dividers to give people any pri-
vacy. There was just one long board with
eight holes cut into it and rolls of toilet
paper near each hole to remind you where you
were as if the foul smell of the place didn't
do it for you. I'd used outhouses in Georgia
when I was a kid visiting my Grandma Crews, so
I knew what they were like. I'd just never
seen an outhouse so big! That made me appreciate the Air Force accomodations at Bien Hoa
even more.
At least at Bien Hoa we didn't have to smell
burning human waste, like the guys here did.
The back walls of the outhouses here had hin-
ged doors. Behind each door at ground-level
was one half of a steel drum that once held a
petroleum product of one type or another. The
human waste would collect in these containers
and some unlucky person was put on a burning
detail to get rid of the waste. They would
pull the containers outside by hand. Then

they'd pour some diesel fuel all over the
human waste, stir it around with a big strong
stick and then pour some gas on it. The fuel
was then lit and as the stuff burned, every
once in awhile, the unfortunate individual on
the detail would have to stir the stuff
around and maybe add more fuel until it all
burned away. The fires always emitted dark
stinking smoke and you had to hope the wind
(if there was any) would blow the stink and
smoke away from wherever you happened to be.
The shuttle bus I was on one day drove right
through the smoke of a burning outhouse waste
container so I can tell you first-hand how
terrible the smell is. That was one extra
work detail I'm glad I never had to be on.

That night five of us went to a service
club at Long Binh and had a buffet-style meal
and then listened to a live band play for
awhile. You can't beat good food, good music
and good friends for an enjoyable evening.

Christmas morning we hitched a ride the
few miles from my friend's barracks across
the base to where the ampitheater was. Long
Binh was a huge Army base. Even though we
got there early, around 8:20 a.m., the place
filled up quickly. At first, we were fairly
close to the stage, to the right of it. We
couldn't sit in front of it because rows of
folding metal chairs had been set up there
for the high-ranking people and wounded GIs
who were being driven in buses from the hospital. Then a bunch of Army "grunts" (infantry) just arriving straight from the
field with mud still on their boots and uniforms told us that we had to move to another
location because this area was reserved for
their unit. We did the smart thing and moved. Even without their weapons, they were a
lot bigger and tougher than us and out-num-
bered us by about 5 or 6 to 1. Yep, we
definitely did the right thing. We ended up
so far away from the stage that when I got

my film developed showing people on stage,
they looked like little ants. You couldn't
tell who was Bob Hope and who was Jim Nabors
in my pictures.

It was the most awsome show I'd ever seen
in my life. To find out that I'd gotten to
see, in person and not on TV, the last show
Bob Hope did during the war in Vietnam made
it even more special. I also found out later
that the three of us from Bien Hoa were the
only people from my unit who got to go and
see it. Talk about lucky!

I'd also brought my tape recorder with me
and a couple of blank cassette tapes. I recorded most of the show, filling up both
sides of the two tapes. When I loaned them
to a friend to listen to at Clark Air Base a
few years later, I never got them back. A
big piece of history was now gone forever.
Like Bob Hope sang, "Thanks for the memories!"

Martha Raye came on stage near the end of
the show and surprised Bob Hope because she
wasn't traveling with his USO show. The
words she spoke to the crowd of almost 25,000
GIs will never be forgotten. "People back
home care more about you over here than you
could ever know. The dissenters and draft-
dodgers and people like them in the U.S.
could never in God's world be worthy enough
to shine your boots, and don't you ever forget it!" We gave her a standing ovation that
lasted for awhile.

Bob Hope said something similar. "Don't
pay any attention to draft-dodgers or dissenters. Take a good look at one of them and
ask yourself, what did he ever do for his
country?"

When a female singer took the stage and
asked everyone to join her in singing "Silent
Night," after a few lines I looked around the
crowd. There were lots of guys with tears in
their eyes, myself included. I'd never seen
grown men cry before, especially surprised

that these battle-hardened grunts near us
were. The NBC cameras that were recording
the show for TV audiences back in the States
couldn't give this live show justice. It
was by far the biggest and most entertaining
thing I'd ever experienced in my life. God
bless you Bob Hope and Martha Raye! Sadly,
they're both dead now but my memory of them
lives on.

That ampitheater was so hot, I took my
shirt off. Big mistake! I ended up with
the worst sunburn that I've ever had, before or since. I was in agony for days. My
roommate did the same thing and suffered for
it too. What is that saying, "Misery loves
company?" We both were miserable for a
week.

The mail I got that week had both good
news and bad. I got a letter from my West
Georgia College roommate. He told me that
he was getting married in the summer of 1972.
That was the good news. The bad news came
from my family's landlord in Gossmansdorf,
West Germany. Her father died on December
3rd. We called him Opa (German for grand-
father). He was a World War I veteran.

On December 26th I wrote home and told my
parents how lucky I'd been for getting to see
the Bob Hope show at Long Binh. That was
worth writing home about. I also went to the
dispensary to get something for my sunburn.
It hurt so bad, I had to sleep on my stomach
and try not to move my head from side to
side. They gave me some Tetracaine Ointment
to put on it three times a day for three or
four days.

My parents sent me a can of cookies for
Christmas and I shared some with my roommates. They were so light and tasty and the
can kept them from being broken into pieces.

Around this time in December, I collected
on a bet I'd made, the second bet I'd won recently. Both bets had to do with when the

base would get attacked. I'd bet $1.00 that
we'd get hit before the 25th and we did,
twice!

I found out that while I'd been enjoying
myself at the Bob Hope USO show, my fellow
Passenger Service co-workers had worked over
30 planes and 4,275 passengers in a few
hours. They told me that a few times, just
to rub it in. I didn't feel guilty at all,
but rather lucky as can be. I thanked my
supervisor for letting me go to the Bob Hope
show and told him I'd work extra hard for him
to show my gratitude.

As 1971 was coming to an end, only 157,000
American GIs remained in Vietnam. The 1st
Cavalry Division (Airmobile) still had units
operating across the flightline from us.
Down the road from them a short distance was
a compound with Navy Seabees. They were
packing up and getting ready to leave soon.
Our own unit was steadily shrinking too.
Rumors were still going around about a possible early PCS (Permanent Change of Station)
for the rest of us still here in Detachment 5
8th Aerial Port Squadron.

There had been a cease-fire agreed to by
the Viet Cong and South Vietnam's armed
forces and the U.S. during Christmas and
again for our New Year. We were hoping that
it would remain peaceful and quiet here so we
could celebrate the holidays and live to tell
about it.

I had to work on the last day of 1971. At
11:45   that night, I wrote my last letter
home for that year and wished my parents and
two brothers a happy new year. I'd had a
good Christmas and in addition to gifts I'd
received from home, I got some at the club at
Long Binh Army Base. Some organizations in
the States had sent red and green cloth bags
full of goodies to the troops in Vietnam. I
got a red cloth bag containing nail clippers,

a comb, a deck of cards, candy, a ball pen
and some other things that I can't recall.

   1971 had been a year full of many changes
for me. I'd begun the year as a college
student on the campus of West Georgia College
in Carrollton, Georgia. At the end of my
second year in June, I'd enlisted in the Air
Force and went to Texas for basic training
and tech school. Then I took a month of
leave back home in Sharpsburg, Georgia after
finding out I was going to Vietnam. I got to
Bien Hoa Air Base in October and since November we'd been attacked three times and I got
to see the very last Bob Hope Christmas
Special ever performed in Vietnam. What a
year!

CHAPTER FOUR

JANUARY 1972

My roommates and I celebrated the arrival of 1972 by attending a cookout down by the detachment bar. We played a few games of pool in the bar and toasted the new year with a few drinks with some friends. I don't remember what time we left the bar. When we got back to our barracks, somebody challenged us to a shaving cream and wet towel fight. We joined a bunch of other guys doing that until 2 a.m. We had a lot of fun and nobody got hurt, but what a mess!

I don't know how I got to work the next morning on time but I did. I didn't drink coffee at all then and I managed to work my 12-hour shift with less sleep than I normally got. Being young and healthy probably had a lot to do with it, I'm sure. The new year began on a good note and the workload was lighter too.

My LES (Leave and Earnings Statement) for December showed that with the new pay raise, my pay was now $396.00 per month. I was really looking forward to February when I would be promoted to A1C (Airman First Class or E-3). I'd get $409.00 a month then. Wow, a whopping $13.00 a month pay raise! If I got a stateside assignment after leaving here I'd get $74.00 less per month. That's because I'd be losing my hostile fire and overseas duty pay. I had a college student loan to pay off, so pay was always on my mind.

Now I was starting to understand the arguments for staying here for a second tour that some guys made to those of us who questioned their sanity. "What? Stay here another year? Are you insane?" For example, one guy put it like this. It was safer here than it was on the highways back in the States. A

person could get killed in a car accident any
day of the week there but here, the chances
of getting even slightly hurt were much less.
The numbers of highway deaths in the U.S. ex-
ceeded the number of deaths in Vietnam during
the previous year. He had a valid point.

One thing I noticed right away in January
1972 was the higher prices of stuff sold in
the BX. In December, a stereo I saw sold for
$65.00 and the same one now sold for $72.00.
My camera film went up $2.00 more and I still
had no flashcubes for it after waiting a
month and a half.

I'd been talking to some of the Seabees
that were stationed near Bien Hoa. One of
their high-ranking CPOs (Chief Petty Officer)
told me that they had orders and MTAs to fly
out of Tan Son Nhut Air Base in Saigon in a
few days, others in a few weeks. Most of
them were ready to go right now and were doing nothing but sitting around waiting. He
said that if I could help them fly out of
Bien Hoa now instead of Tan Son Nhut later,
they would give me several window air conditioners from their buildings to use in our
barracks. They'd been told that they were
going to turn over their entire compound and
everything in it to the Vietnamese military.
He said they'd rather give the stuff to other
Americans to use instead of giving it to the
Vietnamese. After all, he said, American
taxpayers paid for the stuff. He also
sweetened the deal with some wooden seachests full of office supplies which were
brought over the day after I told him I'd get
his men out through Bien Hoa a few at a time.

We never were able to get any air conditioners though because their boss wouldn't
allow them to be removed for fear that the
Vietnamese would get upset when the facilities were officially turned over to them and
the buildings were found to be un-air con-

ditioned. The office supplies and large
wooden seachests with metal handles at both
ends were much appreciated though.

A friend and I borrowed our unit's only
pickup truck and drove over to the Seabee
camp one day to get some of the promised
stuff because they couldn't deliver all of it
to us. We returned with a load of wooden
seachests, or footlockers as we called them.
We got a lot of office supplies too, but sadly, no air conditioners. Well, at least I
kept up my end of the bargain. It sure
would have been nice to have an air conditioned room in the barracks.

I was fascinated by all the different
types of planes and helicopters that were at
Bien Hoa, either just passing through or
stationed here. Some had been flying since
World War II, like the C-47 belonging to the
Navy that I photographed here one day.
Another plane that used to belong to the
Navy but now had the markings of the VNAF
was a Korean War left-over. It had a couple
of different nicknames. One was "Spad" and
another was "Sandy." It was the A-1 Skyraider, a propeller-driven fighter/bomber
that flew off of U.S. Navy aircraft carriers
during the Korean War. There were both
single seaters and two seater versions here.
The U.S. government also gave South Vietnam lots of Cessna A-37 Dragonfly fighter/
bombers. Many were stationed here along
with F-5 Freedom Fighters. Both aircraft
were powered by two jet engines. Other aircraft we gave to the VNAF that I saw here
were: C-123 Provider, a twin engine, propeller-driven cargo plane; Cessna O-1 Bird-
dog which was a single engine, propeller-
driven spotter plane; CH-47 Chinook helicopter that had two engines and could carry
a large load of troops and cargo; UH1H
"Huey" helicopter for carrying troops and

strafing enemy forces with machine guns and
rockets. We also gave them the C-118 "Flying Boxcar" or "Flying Coffin" as some
people called it. It was first used in the
Korean War and was older than some of the
pilots who flew it.

I never saw any C-5 transports at Bien
Hoa. The runway here was either too short
or it couldn't take the weight of the giant
"Galaxy". The oddest plane I saw at Bien
Hoa was a C-124 Globemaster cargo plane. It
had four propellers and was nicknamed "Old
Shakey." It was flown here by members of
the Oklahoma Air National Guard. What really
got my attention was the elevator at the
back of the plane. It dropped straight down
to the ground from near the tail, which was
high off the ground. Then the nose of the
plane opened up, split down the middle with
a left half and a right half. They were
called "clam shell" doors. After they opened up all the way, a ramp lowered to the
ground and vehicles could drive right off
the plane, out the front and onto the
ground.

January 10, 1972 was a very busy day for
me. I processed three commercial flights,
the most I'd ever done during one shift. A
base just a few miles from here got attacked
that day. I could hear the shooting and a
story about it was in the newspaper soon
afterwards. I was glad it was somebody
else getting hit and not us.

The next day I wrote a letter home during
a short break I got at work. It was a short
letter because soon after starting it, I got
busy when some guys on emergency leave showed up. I had to help them get on a flight
out of here.

One of those guys was in the Army and to
pass the time, he told me a few things about

the Viet Cong, who GIs often referred to as
"Charlie." He said that he and members of his
unit sometimes found 122mm rockets that had
been set up to be fired. He told me that the
VC were smart because they'd use timers on the
rockets. That way, if we were able to detect
where the rockets had been fired from, the VC
were long gone. They aimed the rockets, set
the timers, then left the area.

Some guys in my unit told me how nice the
BX and other facilities at Tan Son Nhut Air
Base in Saigon were compared to what we had
here. One day I decided that I just had to
go there and see for myself. I got a pass
authorizing me to travel there and back. I
rode on the Army shuttle bus that Saturday
morning. The bus made stops at the 1st Cav
area on the other side of Bien Hoa from where
I worked. It then stopped at the Seabee compound down the road from the 1st Cav. Next
it stopped at USARV Headquarters at Long Binh
Army Base. The last stop was at MACV Headquarters across the street from Tan Son Nhut.
The air base had 3-wheeled Lambretta
motorized vehicles with a driver up front and
a passenger compartment in back. The passengers sat facing across from eachother on
bench seats along both sides of the vehicle.
These were the base taxis that would take you
anywhere on base for a low flat fee.
The BX at Tan Son Nhut was huge. Right
next to it was a large movie theater. Not
far from there was a big all-ranks club with
go-go girls dancing in cages. They even had
a BX concession office where you could look
through brochures on new cars and even order
a new car from there to be delivered to the
States near whatever airport you flew into.
The salesman there told me all about how
to order a new car but since I still had a
lot of time left on my tour and didn't have
travel orders to a stateside base, which was

a requirement for the GI discount, I could
only dream about owning a new car one day.
My friends at Bien Hoa were right. This
place was much nicer.

The Army shuttle bus had all of the side
windows covered with heavy-duty metal
screens. I was told it was to prevent anyone from throwing a hand grenade into the
bus. It stayed on the main roads all the
time. Some of the roads were two lanes but
most that we drove on were four lanes, with
wall-to-wall traffic. It's a wonder we did-
n't run into or over anyone as our bus was
just about the largest vehicle on the road.
The only other two large vehicles I saw that
trip had a head-on collision. Two big dump
trucks crashed and caused a major traffic
jam. People in Saigon didn't pay any attention to the separate lanes on each side of
the road. They took up any space they
could find to drive in even if they straddl-
ed two lanes at the same time. It was pure
chaos!

I managed to take some pictures through
the big front window of the bus. Parts of
Saigon looked like an Oriental city you'd
expect to see in Asia. Other parts looked
like Paris, France. When the French were
here, they had a big influence on the way
some roads and buildings were constructed.
A lot of French-manufactured cars were still
in use as taxis, colored blue and yellow.
Small motorcycles and mopeds competed for
space in the traffic and none of the two-
wheeled riders wore helmets for protection.

Some of the Vietnamese I saw in Saigon
wore western-style clothes and others wore
traditional Vietnamese clothes including
the conical straw hats and black pants.
When we crossed one river, it stank like an
open sewer and was pure black. I saw
houses built on stilts right over that
river and I couldn't understand how they

stood the smell.

Except for the dump trucks crashing, my
trip was uneventful. The pictures I took on
that excursion turned out real good. I'd
used an instamatic camera with color film.

On January 12, 1972 VC sappers attacked
Bien Hoa Air Base. I found out about the
attack from some of the Army and Air Force
MPs and SPs that came into the passenger terminal and nearby snack bar on a daily basis.
Some of them were dog handlers. Some of the
dogs sniffed passenger baggage for drugs and
some of them were patrol dogs, out to bite
any VC that might be trying to sneak into the
base at night like some did last night.

Two VC sappers got through the base de-
fenses on the Vietnamese side of the base at
around 4 a.m. They blew up a supply building
and one of them got away. The other one was-
n't so lucky. He set off two Claymore mines
and got blown up in the explosions.

Coincidentally, just the day before, some
sappers blasted a government office in
Saigon. We had no idea if there was a connection between the two attacks but it did put
us on edge. It gave notice once again that
the Viet Cong were capable of striking when
and where they wanted to, at least to some
degree.

For three days in a row, January 14, 15 and
16, 1972 the Army units at Bien Hoa were
attacked. The units were on the other side of
the runway from the Air Force units. The 1st
Cavalry Division units there had helicopters
and artillery within a couple of miles of our
barracks, plus fuel storage and munitions
storage areas. They were a big target for the
enemy.

On one of those three days, the ammo dump
at the 1st Cav area got hit. The blast was so
powerful it woke me up early that morning. My
room shook a lot too. I'd never heard or felt

anything that loud and powerful before, especially considering that it was coming from
a couple of miles away. Our siren didn't go
off so I knew we weren't being attacked.

After I got to work that morning, some
guys told me they had gone outside to see if
they could see anything and they could see
flames shooting over a couple of hundred
feet up.

There were some Army MPs that had an office inside the terminal where I worked.
They were in charge of Customs, making sure
nobody took anything that was illegal from
Vietnam back to the States with them like
drugs or weapons. They had contacted their
friends over in the 1st Cav area and said
the PX (Post Exchange - the Army equivalent
of an Air Force BX) and a helicopter repair
hanger had gotten blown up along with an
ammo storage warehouse. They weren't sure
if sappers had done it or mortar rounds, as
it was still being investigated. Some
people got injured but nobody died in the
explosions. The other two attacks over
there this week were random rocket and mortar hits with little damage to anything.
These were typical harrassment tactics used
by the Viet Cong. They weren't trying to
take over a base or destroy a fighting unit
in a battle. They were just letting us know
that they could do stuff like that just
about any time they wanted to.

The last time they tried to take over Bien
Hoa in force was during the 1968 Tet Offensive. Their forces were decimated by our
firepower. They never tried that again.

Sometime during the middle of January I
got a notice saying my AFSC (Air Force Specialty Code which is used to identify your
career field, similar to an Army MOS) was
changing from 60530 to 60550 retroactive to
January 1, 1972. I was originally supposed

to have taken the final test for my career
field correspondence course before Christmas.
I still had not taken it yet even though I
passed the NCOIC interview-questioning. I had
no idea how I could have been awarded my 5-
skill level before I even passed the last
closed book test.

We heard a lot of small-arms fire that went
on seemingly for hours one night the week of
January 17, 1972. It sounded like it was
coming from the 1st Cav area. Nothing happened on the Air Force side of Bien Hoa during
that time and boy were we glad of that!

One of my friends in the barracks I was in
had a reel-to-reel tape deck stereo system
with really nice speakers. The music coming
from his stereo sounded much better than
mine. He could listen to many hours of music
continuously, with or without headphones on.
I was a little envious but I knew I couldn't
afford a set-up as nice as that.

On January 21, 1972 at around 3 a.m., a blast
more powerful than the one I'd heard and felt
only a week ago woke me up from a sound
sleep. Once again, an ammo storage area on
the Army side of Bien Hoa got hit. The barracks shook, my bed shook, and I woke up right
away. For some reason I yelled, "Hit the
deck! Hit the deck! Hit the deck!" real
loud. My roommate in the top bunk came
crashing down on top of me and on John's leg
as well. John and I must have reached the
floor between our two beds at the same time
for that to have happened. It looked like a
scene from a Three Stooges movie with Curly,
Moe and Larry all arriving at the same place
at the same time. All three of us got banged up and sore as we sought cover under the
beds.
We found out the next day that Armand

broke a foot when he jumped down from his top
bunk onto John's leg.

The neighbor across the hall told me that
it was my yelling, "Hit the deck!" that woke
him up and not the explosion or shaking of
the building. We all thought it was strange
that the enemy knew exactly where the Army's
ammo dump was and that they were able to blow
it up again. Of course we had no idea that
the Army may have had more than one ammo dump
in the general area of the other one that was
previously blown up. Still, two huge explosions in one week was not normal around here.

One thing that I was learning about the
Air Force was that it was good to have
friends who had friends that worked in different places. A friend of mine talked to a
friend of his who worked in CBPO (Consolidated Base Personnel Office) one day. He
said that his friend saw some paperwork about
three guys from our detachment that were going to be sent to Clark Air Base in the Philippines and that my name was one of them.
That information caused us to suspect even
more than before that we might all be leaving
Bien Hoa before our year-long tour was up.
Since the paperwork wasn't actual assignment
orders for a PCS (Permanent Change of Station)
we didn't know when I and the other two guys
would be leaving. Talk about suspense!

On one of my days off shortly after getting that news, a friend and I and a fellow
tech school classmate went to the base gym
and got in a basketball game. I played on a
team with a bunch of guys I didn't know and
my two friends ended up on the other team.
My team won 50 to 46. We'd agreed at the
start that the first team to score 50 points
was the winner.

We played with no time-outs and in the
heat of the day. That was some game! The

gym had a roof and one walled side, two sides
being fences and one side was completely open.
At least we had some shade to play in. I
wished I'd brought my swimming trunks along
because the base swimming pool was right next
to the gym and after the basketball game was
over, I felt like jumping into the pool to
cool off some.

Sometime in January I got a letter from
home and was told that my cousin, Mike Crews,
was now in the Army and had left for Vietnam
on January 16th or 17th. On January 20th, we
had a flight from McGuire Air Force Base that
landed here and if I'd known he was on it, I
could have welcomed him here. I never did
see him and didn't know what his address was.
He and I used to hang out together a lot on
the weekends I'd spent at his house in Hogan-
sville, Georgia when I was a student at West
Georgia College. I know Mike survived his
tour of duty because he died in a car wreck
in Georgia around 1989.

My stereo quit working one day and there
was no place on base to bring it for repairs.
On January 28th I took it to the stereo repair shop at Long Binh Army Base. It would
stay there for awhile because they had to order a part.
I received 13 letters from friends and
relatives during the third week of January.
When I wrote to my parents on the 29th, that
was the first letter I'd written to anyone in
a week.
I finally took the closed-book test for my
CDCs. There were 62 multiple-choice questions and it only took a half hour to complete it. I felt very confident that I'd
scored at least 90% on it but I later found
out that I passed with a lower score than
that.
I went back to CBPO again to see about

cross training into the administrative field
because of a change of heart about staying
overseas. They told me at CBPO that it
would be impossible for me to get stationed
back in the States in my current career
field. That was because there were only
nine bases that used my AFSC and there were
no openings at any of them. I was also told
that I'd been in Vietnam over three months,
the limit for cross training. However, I
might be able to cross train into the military police or fire fighting career fields
because of shortages in those two. At least
for awhile I'd be staying in my present
career field and staying overseas, possibly
going to the Philippines.

We had a Commander's Call at the end of
January and there had been no mention of
promotions for any of the airmen in our detachment. That caused me to believe that I
wouldn't get my second stripe until March 1.
Either that or CBPO hadn't gotten the promotion list to our commander prior to Commander's Call.

In order to be prepared for a possible
Tet Offensive like that of 1968 when Bien
Hoa was hit by 124 rockets, mortars and a
ground attack, we were issued gun cards and
instructions on what to do if we got attacked. Everyone had to take a turn at guard
duty now too from 9p.m. to 6a.m. Two people
from the detachment got an M-16, a helmet
and flak jacket and became security police
augmentees. There was a different team
formed each night for guard duty. So far
my name had not appeared on the list.

An accident caused me to get a tetanus
shot and a bandaid. One day while in my
barracks I got hungry and decided to eat a
can of lasagna. I had traded some things

with an Army friend of mine for a case of C-
rations. I was one of only a few people that
actually liked those meals that came in little
green cans. Yes, even the ham and lima beans.
I used my P-38, the world's smallest can open-
er to open the can and there was just a tiny
bit of metal still holding the lid to the
rest of the can. When I pulled the lid off, I
pulled too hard and my ring finger of my
right hand got cut somehow. It bled a lot and
I went to the dispensary. I didn't have to
get any stitches but the shot gave me a fever
and a headache. I was given half a day off
and went to bed and slept for awhile.

My roommate during my second year at West
Georgia College sent me a clipping from the
campus newspaper. It was an article about
what would happen if your grade point average
fell below 1.9. You had to drop out of college for a year and you'd be re-classified
from 2-S (student deferrment) to 1-A (draft
eligible). I made a joke about it. Maybe
they could join me here in Vietnam and major
in Southeast Asian Studies for that year.

Since the price of film increased so much
for the camera I'd bought from that helicopter
door gunner, I ended up buying another camera
in the BX. It was an instamatic camera that
used the "X" magic flashcube without batteries
for only $18.00 and that included color film
and a flashcube. It took very good color
pictures.

The rumor going around now was that we'd be
out of Vietnam by June or July. It wasn't
official but it was getting evident by the
movements on base and people leaving. Also,
there was a lot of talk, all speculation,
about whether or not Saigon would be going
off-limits because of Tet and what happened
in 1968.

My future was so unsure at this point in
time. I may or may not be staying in my
career field. I may or may not get another

overseas assignment. I may or may not get
to leave here in June or July. I may or may
not get promoted to A1C (Airman First Class)
when I thought I would. Everything seemed
to be "maybe this, maybe that" back then.

Our politicians and the generals that
worked for them always tried to make things
seem better than they were, whether it was
by what they said on TV or to newspaper re-
porters. They had me believing that we were
winning the war and that was the reason why
we were all leaving. As history has proven,
their words didn't match the reality of what
was really happening.

I'm surprised that I didn't gain any
weight during the time I worked day shift.
Many lunch breaks were spent eating food
from the terminal snack bar and either eating there or in my office and I almost always got the same thing each day. I ate two
chili dogs with french fries and a soda to
wash it down. On the few trips to the chow
hall, which had to be made in a vehicle because it was so far from the passenger terminal, I'd get some hamburgers and fries. I
guess those basketball games and the heat
and humidity helped keep the pounds off.

January 30, 1972 started out just like
every other day here, warm, sunny and boring. The workload was easing up some with
fewer flights in and out. I had no idea
why. The day ended up anything but boring.
That night we got our first ground attack
since my arrival here last October.

It was a Sunday night, around 9:30 p.m. I
was in my room and a neighbor pounded on the
door while yelling loudly that we were being
attacked. Some friends and I went outside
and saw flares everywhere along the base
perimeter on our side of the base. It seemed like some of them were about 100 yards
away, slowly drifting downward by parachute,

brightly turning night into day. Some
appeared to be landing near the area not too
far from where some planes carrying inbound
cargo were off-loaded by the cargo handling
people of our detachment. That gave one of
my friends an idea. We talked about what a
great souvineer those parachutes would make
and how we could get some. But first, we had
to wait until the shooting stopped and it was
safe for us to put our plan into action.

As the three of us were standing outside
near the road that went past our barracks, we
saw a security policeman with a German Sheppard jogging down the road heading towards
the perimeter of the base. There were sandbagged defensive positions nearby. I asked
him if he knew what was going on. He said
some VC had gotten through the wire and were
on the base. We found out later that that
was not the case.

After telling us that, we went over to the
squadron bar two buildings down from ours and
closer to the perimeter fence. At first, the
shooting was sporadic but got heavier after a
few minutes. There were machine guns and
small arms firing, with tracers glowing in
the darkness going into and out of the base.
Red tracers from American weapons split the
darkness and bounced off some tin roofs of
the buildings in Bien Hoa City nearest to the
base. That's where the incoming gunfire was
coming from, right across the open field
from where we were.

Some of the flares that had been lighting
up the night sky landed in the dry grass and
started some fires in between the base and
the outskirts of Bien Hoa City. We could see
more security police with their M-16s arriving near the sandbagged fighting positions
not far from us. People over there and here
by the barracks were ducking for cover.

My friends and I went up the steps to the
second floor of a nearby barracks to get a

better view of the fighting. We weren't
there long because the first sergeant and the
detachment commander saw us as they ran from
building to building. They were telling
everyone to get inside and stay inside and to
put our helmets and flak jackets on. On the
way back down the steps, we could see helicopters flying over the area between the
base and the city. They had powerful search-
lights on, trying to spot the enemy gunners.

After things quieted down, my friend and
I went down to where the warehouse tugs were
parked, outside of the passenger terminal.
We rode a short distance to where we'd spotted some of the parachute flares land but we
couldn't get a single one. The wind blew
them into the perimeter wire, or very close
to it. We knew there were mines and trip
flares in that area so we stayed away from
there.

There were no casualties on base from the
gunfire coming into it. I think only a few
VC were involved in the incident and doubt
that they intended on doing anything other
than harass the base just to show us that
they could shoot at us any time they wanted
to. Or, they could have been providing a
diversion to get our defensive forces focused
on this side of the base while they tried
something on the other side. We'll never
know.

That was the first time in my life that I
had ever seen tracer rounds fired and it not
be on TV or in a movie. My friends and I
found it kind of exciting even though it was
dangerous. We should have stayed inside of
our barracks instead of going outside when
bullets were flying into and out of the base.
Yes, we were young and dumb, with the empha-
sis on dumb; fearless just enough to be
stupid. That's the way I feel about it now.

The next day, the attack was all everybody was talking about. At least until some

of us were told to report to the Orderly Room.
That's where the First Sergeant's office was.
I was afraid that I was in trouble for being
outside when the attack was going on. With
that on my mind, I was surprised to see a lot
of others in the Orderly Room, crowded around
the First Sergeant's desk. When I reported in
to him, he held out his hand and said, "Con-
gratulations!" With his other hand, he gave
me copies of my promotion orders, dated 31
January 1972. It took me awhile to find my
own name on them. It was on the back. Twenty
three guys in my unit were promoted to A1C
(Airman First Class, E-3) on the same day.

Special Order AB-3. Paragraph 5: Each of
the following Airmen, Det. 5, 8th APSq, this
station, is promoted to the permanent grade of
AIRMAN FIRST CLASS, effective and with date of
rank 1 Feb. 72. Authority: AFR 39-29. There
on the back, fifth from the bottom of the list
that carried over from the front, underlined
with a blue marker: CREWS, STEPHEN A. Boy,
was I happy! Happy to not be in trouble and
happy to get promoted and get a pay raise.

With that new set of stripes, I started a
tradition. I sewed on a set of stripes myself
and the tailor shop did the rest of them. I
sewed on stripes all through my Air Force
career, one set by hand with each promotion,
to signify all the hard work I put into earn-
ing each stripe along the way.

I was so excited to get promoted that as
soon as I got a chance, I wrote a letter home
to tell my family. Only eight more months
and I'd be eligible to be promoted to Sergeant.
I also told my family that I'd been to CBPO
and found out that I was going to Clark Air
Base, Philippines from here, unofficially of
course. I had no orders to go there yet.

I guess I was just a sucker for stray dogs.
I found another one just wandering around and
when I called it, it came over to me. I knew
somebody had taken good care of it because he

had a rabies shot tag on a collar and looked
healthy. I decided to call him "Blue" because of the song I'd heard on the radio that
week about a dog named Blue. My roommates
said it was OK with them to keep the dog in
the livingroom.

My roommates were making plans to go on
an R & R trip together to Hawaii. I was
thinking about going to either there or
Austrailia or Bangkok, Thailand. I was even
considering taking 14 days of leave and just
staying here and save some money. They later
decided to take a regular leave and fly all
the way home.
     One day one of my friends showed me a lot
of pictures he'd taken during his R & R to
Thailand. He told me a lot about all the
things he'd seen and all the tourist attractions he'd gone to as well. He ended up
giving me dozens of pictures he'd taken
there and after seeing and hearing so much
about it, I decided that I'd rather go to a
place that nobody I knew had gone to and
that was Austrailia. It was still on the
list of R & R centers we could go to, along
with Bangkok, Singapore, Taipei, Manila and
Honolulu. Sydney, Austrailia also had something those other places didn't have, except
for Honolulu. That something was women with
round eyes and white skin and they spoke
English as their native language, even if it
was with an accent.

CHAPTER FIVE

FEBRUARY 1972

All of the units still at Bien Hoa by this
time had down-sized just like we had. The
security police unit now needed help from
other units in doing some of their jobs, like
stringing up barbed wire around defensive
positions and rigging trip flares. I got
selected from my unit one day to be an augmentee to the SPs (Security Police) who were
putting up concertina-style barbed wire and
trip flares in between the runway and taxi
way. It was supposed to be a one day detail
but I ended up helping them for three days.
I didn't mind though. We worked from 7 AM to
3:30 PM. I got sunburned even though I kept
my shirt on, but not as badly as I had back
in December.

I didn't get around to writing another
letter home until the 14th of February. I
told my parents about my three day detail
with the SPs and how I ended up with a few
scratches on my left arm from the barbed
wire. It was a good thing they had provided
me with leather gloves or my hands would have
gotten cut for sure in addition to my arm. I
also told them how we'd put up several thou-
sand yards of coiled barbed wire, stacked
three layers high, in the form of a pyramid.
I also helped them put in trip flares but
they had me stay far away from them when they
set up the claymore mines. They said that
they expected a big attack here this year but
so far nothing had happened at all in comparison to Tet 1968. Only larger bases in
the northern part of South Vietnam had been
hit so far, like Da Nang, Pleiku and Cam Ranh
Bay.

I told my parents that waiting for Tet was
like watching storm clouds in Oklahoma in the
Spring. A tornado may or may not form but
everybody was edgy anyway. We'd lived there

in the early 1960s.

On February 15, 1972 I found out that we would start working an 8-hour shift the next day and I'd be on the 11p.m.to 7a.m.shift. The workload had lightened up and some people were being moved to other offices to gain experience in other areas of their career fields. Nobody knew if this was going to be temporary or not. I thought that it would be just temporary as every week it seemed that something was being changed because of our constant loss of people in the detachment and the workload lightening up as well.

The worst thing about not having as many people in the unit as before was that those of us who remained were given extra details more frequently to help out other units. For example, on February 18th, I had KP (Kitchen Police) in the chow hall from 4:30a.m.to 8 p.m. Two other guys in my detachment had KP each day for a week because of the Tet holiday and lack of civilian help. The Vietnamese civilians who worked on base would start back to work on the following Saturday of next week because of their Tet holiday schedule, so we were told.

There was a 24-hour truce from 6p.m.February 14th to 6p.m.February 15th. It stayed peaceful and I got lucky at the chow hall. After serving sausage and French toast for only one hour, the Vietnamese who worked there showed up and I was told that I could leave.

What I couldn't understand was, why my detachment never got any help from another unit when we were working 12-hour shifts and getting one day off every eight or nine days. We had only one person in a lot of offices doing the work of two people sometimes, like I did, and nobody from another unit augmented our thinned-out workforce.

Another thing I couldn't understand was

why our M-16s and ammunition was locked up in
a metal Conex container in the Air Freight
warehouse when we had that ground attack. If
the VC or North Vietnamese had gotten into
the base that night, they could have killed a
lot of us unarmed people easily enough.
There weren't enough security police to hold
off a concerted attack and the Army wasn't
defending our part of the perimeter at Bien
Hoa, though they did have helicopter gunships
nearby. That's the reason some friends and I
decided to arm ourselves with knives in the
barracks since we weren't allowed to defend
ourselves with guns. If the enemy got in between us in the barracks and where the guns
were locked up several blocks away, we'd be
in trouble.

One guy had the idea to use a lighter and
a can of hair spray and use it like a blow-
torch or flamethrower if any bad guys got into our barracks. We were determined not to
go out without a fight. Luckily, it never
came to that. Still, we had to figure out
ways to defend ourselves and get around the
ridiculous restrictions put on us by our own
leaders.

Can you imagine what it would be like if
we all showed up at the same time to draw
weapons at the Conex in the cargo warehouse?
While the base was being attacked, there
would be a long line while someone tried to
check each gun card number against the gun
stock number and then you had to sign a form
accepting the issue of the M-16 and ammo.
The base could have been overrun by the time
most people got through the line!

Someone said things were done that way because during the attack against Bien Hoa during the Tet Offensive in 1968, some Air Force
people accidently got shot by other Air Force
people who didn't properly identify their
targets before shooting. Either that or they
were lousy shots! You don't put everyone's

life in jeopardy by locking up all the weapons far from where they live just because of
accidental shootings. You train the people
better so those incidents won't happen again
and that's how I felt about it.

The day I got off early from KP duty, I
let my supervisor know. That way I wouldn't
get in any trouble if someone saw me somewhere else on base. That didn't work out as
well as I thought it would. I was told to
come in and work the 11p.m.-7a.m. shift so
I went back to the barracks to try and get
some sleep. If I didn't, I'd be staying up
way beyond twenty four hours straight. Sometime during that afternoon someone from work
came to my room and said that I was being
put on the 3p.m.-11 p.m. shift instead of
what I'd been told before. That was because one of the guys in my detachment was
working part-time in the base movie theater.
He asked to be put on the 11 p.m.-7a.m. shift
so he could keep his part-time job. He got
his wish and I got moved around yet again.
Because so many people were having extra
details to do, there was a shortage of
people in some offices, also because of
people on R & R and on leave and we were all
working different jobs besides our own. I
worked in the Dispatch Office for a few
hours one day and at the Passenger Service
Counter for awhile too. On a more positive
note, I was gaining more knowledge and experience in my career field that would benefit me later on in future assignments and on
promotion tests.

I was nearing the half-way point in my
one year tour. If I stayed until April 23rd
then I'd have 181 days in-country and get
credit for an overseas short tour and credit
for a tour of duty in Vietnam. I still had
not heard when I'd be leaving for Clark Air

Base so I just hoped it wouldn't be until
after April 23rd.

On February 17th I was in the BX just looking around and saw a nice looking watch for
$24.00. It was self-winding, had a day and
date calendar and the watch and wrist band was
all silver stainless steel, shock-proof and
water resistant. I bought it but didn't wear
it until I got to my next base later that
year. I didn't want it to get messed up like
the one I was wearing on a daily basis. The
outside of it was all scratched up and the
gold coloring was coming off all over and the
bare places where the gold paint used to be
was turning green. I had to have the crystal
scraped to remove all the scratches on that
part of it. It still kept good time so I kept
wearing it as my "work" watch, saving the new
one for when I wasn't working.
That same day I stopped by the Orderly
Room and signed the papers for my 5-skill
level, making it official. It was retroactive
to January 1, 1972 when I was still an Airman.
Most people didn't get their 5-skill level until they were promoted to A1C. I found out
that my supervisor pushed the paperwork so I
could get it before I left here since it was
possible that I'd be leaving soon. He had
just gotten a line-number for Technical Sergeant and was going to Yokota Air Base, Japan
from here. I respected him a lot because he
really knew every job in Passenger Service,
inside and out, regulations too.

I must have driven my parents crazy back
then, always changing my story about taking
leave and not taking leave and when I might be
leaving Vietnam and how long it might be until
I saw them again. I should have just not mentioned those things at all until things were
certain instead of saying, "maybe this, maybe
that" all the time in my letters.

One of the things I had to do at work when
I was put on the 11 p.m.-7 a.m. shift that I
didn't have to do on the other shifts was a
report that had to be sent out at midnight
each night. I typed it up and addressed it
to PACAF HQ (Pacific Air Force Headquarters)
and MAC HQ (Military Airlift Command Headquarters). I don't remember all of the stuff
that went into the report but it had to do,
at least in part, with the types of passengers we put on aircraft leaving here. For
example, some were going PCS (Permanent
Change of Station), TDY (Temporary Duty), EL
(Emergency Leave) OL (Ordinary Leave) and
things like that.

I carried the completed report to the
message center, which was in a building near
ours, on the flightline side. Their office
was on the ground floor of the two-story
building. They sent out the message to each
agency it was addressed to.

One night, a few minutes before midnight,
I was walking from my Tri-Service ATCO
office near the front of the passenger terminal towards the doorway at the back of the
building to get to the message center. I
had to cross the entire width of the building and walk past two Army MPs. They were
talking to eachother just outside of their
Customs Office. They always had a K-9 (dog
handler) and drug-sniffing dog on duty at
all times. In fact, one of the MPs had a
very large German Shepard sitting next to
him. He was holding the dog's leash in his
hands. The dog had a muzzle on it too so it
couldn't bite anyone.

They were slightly to my right as I began
walking past them with my nightly report.
Without any warning, the dog leaped up on me
and put a big heavy paw on each shoulder. I
got the you-know-what scared out of me! It
almost knocked me over, it was so big.
Thankfully, he had a muzzle on or I really

would have freaked out. The MP just tugged on
the leash and told the dog to sit or heel and
said, "Sorry about that." I was still too
stunned to reply and kept walking. I heard
the two MPs chuckling over the scare their dog
gave me. He darn near gave me a heart attack!
I think the gray hair I found on my head one
day was caused by that big dog jumping up on
me and not from any of the attacks on the
base. I actually mailed that gray hair home
in a letter one day to prove to my parents
that I found one at the young age of twenty.

Ever since that day, I always put a lot of
distance between me and any dogs, leashes or
not, especially those big German Shepards used
by the MPs. I never got within ten feet of
one after that.

There was less work to do at night and it
was a little bit cooler too. It was too dark
on the night shift to take any pictures. That
was the only thing I didn't like about that
shift.

It had been quiet for the last three weeks
since the ground attack on January 30th. We'd
had no rockets, no mortars and no ground
attack either. It was just too good to think
it might last longer. February 21, 1972 was a
Monday. At 3:15 on that morning I heard BAM!
BAM! BAM! I was on the hard cement floor in
no time at all, trying to get under my bed.
The explosions woke me up before the base
siren went off and by the time it was blaring
its attack warning, I was in the safest place
to be, under my bed and next to the wall. I
managed to get out of my lower bunk without
damaging the mosquito net. I'd moved so fast
that I still had my poncho liner wrapped
around me. In these tense situations, a mere
second could be the difference between life
and death. I wanted to live!

I was still on the floor when someone ran

down the hall yelling for all the augmentees
to report to their duty sections. Some
people in our detachment had been tasked with
helping the security police in repelling
attackers and got some training in air base
defense tactics. Because they were being
called on that morning, I thought another
ground attack might be happening.

I found out later that three rockets hit
the base about a mile from our barracks.
Even at that distance, they were really loud,
especially when exploding at night when it's
normally so quiet. Two Air Force sergeants
were wounded bad enough to be hospitalized.
A truck parked near a building by the ammunition repair squadron took a direct hit and
was blown to bits. The two wounded sergeants
were both hit by shrapnel that went through
the walls of the building they were in, near
the one that got the direct hit. I asked
around but nobody knew where the other two
rockets hit.

Another surprise awaited me when I got to
work that day. I got moved to a different
office to work in, again. The best surprise
was the mail I got that week. A classmate of
mine from Wurzburg American High School in
West Germany wrote to me. The last time I'd
seen him was on the campus of Georgia Tech in
Atlanta. He was a student there when I was a
student at West Georgia College, about 35
miles southwest of there. He showed me
around the campus and then we had lunch at a
well-known restaurant, The Varsity, which was
near the Georgia Tech campus.

I also got a letter from my West Georgia
College roommate during my second year there.
My Aunt Francis Crews wrote also, sending me
the addresses of her two youngest sons, my
cousins Mike and Randy. My Grandma Smith, my
mom's mother also wrote to me. One advantage
of being part of a big family and having lots
of friends was getting lots of mail. In Viet-

nam, mail was a very important thing in our
lives. I managed to reply to most letters in
a timely manner.

I wished I could have been back in Georgia
that summer so I could attend my college
roommate's wedding. He told me that he and
his fiancee were getting married right after
final exams in June. They had gotten engaged
last year. He'd introduced me to his fiancee before I'd left West Georgia for the
Air Force.

The actor and singer Sammy Davis, Jr. landed at Bien Hoa on February 22, 1972. He did
some shows at Long Binh Army Base but I had
to work so I wasn't able to see any. I was
in bed when he landed but I saw him on TV on
the 6 o'clock news and saw some of my friends
on TV too.

I worked in the Dispatch Office a couple
of times since the beginning of the year. My
job was to take down flight information from
Traffic Control and pass it on to others con-
nected with handling the passengers and baggage for the flight. It was an easy job but
it could get tedious with several flights a
day. One day we had thirteen flights, with
two of them getting cancelled. That was
above average for both total number of
flights per day and for cancellations.

Valentine's Day was celebrated by GIs in
Vietnam, at least by those who could. The
married men and those with girlfriends back
home could find a card in most military PXs
or BXs. On some of the larger bases, a guy
could even order some flowers for his girl.

I had been writing to a girl I knew from
church. I had driven her to and from a
football game while I was home on leave right
after tech school. She was a cheerleader so
I sat in the bleachers while she did her

cheering with the other cheerleaders. I had
not gone to school there so I didn't know anyone in the stands.

I think that because her family and she
knew my great uncle and his friends and those
people were either related to or were good
friends of my dad, she wrote me back to be
polite. Pen pals were still a popular thing
in those days.

When Valentine's Day drew near, I decided
to send my pen pal some flowers. I appreciated that she took the time to write to me
and the flowers were a token of my apprecia-
tion. The thing that amazed me about our BX
at Bien Hoa was that you could open up a
catalog full of floral arrangements, place an
order and they'd be delivered anywhere in the
U.S. and for a very reasonable fee.

What's really funny about it all was that,
back then, I thought the flowers were actually traveling from some flower shop in Vietnam
all the way to Georgia. I commented to my
parents in a letter when I found out that the
flowers I sent to my pen pal got there in
time. I can't believe I was actually so "in
the dark" about things like that.

Now let me tell you about something that
wasn't so funny. In every war movie I'd ever
seen and in every book about war I'd ever
read, when a person was on guard duty, they
had a gun. How can you guard something without being able to protect whatever it is you'
re guarding, and protect yourself, without a
gun? You can't! On at least three different
occasions in Vietnam, I was put on guard duty
and not given a gun! Each time I had guard
duty, it was at night. That's when the VC
snuck into the base and blew things up.

On February 27, 1972 I had guard duty from
7 to 10 p.m.in our detachment's freight yard.
I was given a flashlight and my instructions
were to walk around with that flashlight and

make sure that nobody stole anything in the
freight yard. A 144 pound 5 foot 8 inch
skinny kid is going to stop someone with a
flashlight? I don't think so! I saw enough
war movies and TV shows like Combat and saw
guards WITH GUNS being killed while on guard
duty. So, I came up with a plan of my own so
I wouldn't end up like any of them. Yes,
they influenced me, but in a good way. I
climbed up on top of the highest crate of
cargo and flashed the light around every few
minutes and hoped I survived the night. I
wasn't about to walk around that freight yard
by myself at night without a gun for protection while on guard duty. No way! Also, I
wasn't given a radio either, so if I saw anything suspicious, I couldn't call for help.
     That's just one example of some of the
stupid things that the higher ranking people
in charge had us lower ranking people do in
Vietnam. They knew that the VC had previously
snuck onto the base and blew things up but yet
they expected us to perform guard duty in a
war zone with only a flashlight.

     I stayed up late on the night of February
27th to see my two roommates leave. They were
going home on a two week leave. Their plane
was supposed to leave at 30 minutes after midnight but didn't leave until 2:45 a.m. I had
worked a shift of guard duty earlier that
night so by the time they left, I was ready to
get some sleep.
     The next day I was told that I'd be getting
my old job back in Tri-Service ATCO because
the guy who was currently working the 11p.m.to
7a.m.shift was going back to the states. His
sister had a miscarriage and the Red Cross
helped him get a compassionate leave to go
home. For the past week I'd been working behind the Passenger Service counter and in the
Dispatch Office. I was losing track of how
many times I was moved from place to place and

shift to shift. Well, it still beat living
in the mud as some GIs had to do almost
every day as part of their jobs.

The drug problem in Vietnam wasn't the
only problem the military establishment had
to deal with. There were 242,896 AWOL (Absent Without Official Leave) incidents and
98,059 deserters listed by the U.S. military
forces in Vietnam during 1972. As if that
wasn't a bad enough indicator of low morale
and discipline, "fragging" incidents were
increasing. A "fragging" is where a military member, usually an enlisted person,
throws or places a hand grenade in the quarters of another military member, usually an
officer. In just the first eight months of
1971, there were 238 "fragging" incidents
reported. That resulted in eleven deaths
and 154 injuries. In the first couple of
months of 1972, so many "fragging" incidents had happened that 86 American GIs died
and hundreds more were injured.

The AWOLs might have been high as a result of some people going AWOL multiple
times, not that there were that many indiv-
iduals gone from their post. In my unit, we
had a drug and venerial disease problem and
a few drunken fights resulting in injuries,
but we didn't have any "fragging" incidents
nor any AWOLs that I'm aware of.

French-built bunker near American-built
movie theater at Bien Hoa Air Base. It
was a French base in the 1950s.

This defensive position was near my
barracks. The fence was put up to keep
hand grenades from being thrown into it.

Sandbagged defensive position at Bien Hoa
near my barracks. Buildings in the distance
are part of Bien Hoa City. Deep cement
drain is just in front of position.

Mortar and rocket attack on November 25, 1971
damaged this aircraft revetment that separate
aircraft from one another and protects them.

On November 25, 1971 a 122mm rocket made this
hole after blowing up a flatbed truck that
had been parked where the hole is.

November 1971 a couple of weeks after my
arrival at Bien Hoa Air Base, Vietnam.

Several people are looking at where a rocket
hit into soft sand the night of December 19,
1971. This was our second attack so far.

Vietnamese F-5 Freedom Fighter damaged in the
attack on Bien Hoa December 19, 1971.

A rocket hit in soft dirt and made a lot of holes in the wall near some aircraft revetments the night of December 19, 1971.

The civil engineers building and tractors in their compound at Bien Hoa got hit hard by rockets late at night on December 19, 1971.

Attack on Bien Hoa August 1, 1972 caused lots
of damage to the back of the passenger terminal and killed a GI inside near the wall.

Our unit's only truck got holed at head-
level in the cab on August 1, 1972.

A C-7 Caribou with its rear cargo door blown
off, tires flattened and fuel tanks punctured.

An RB-77 with flattened tires. Both planes
were hit at Bien Hoa August 1, 1972.

Bien Hoa Air Base dispensary damaged in the attack on August 1, 1972.

Bien Hoa chapel had back windows blown out and curtains burned on August 1, 1972.

Damaged beer and soda storage lot at Bien Hoa
August 1,1972. Shells just missed the BX on
the other side of the lot.

This drainage ditch flowed with beer and soda
from the damaged supplies on the left. The
white fence on right was behind base chapel.

On August 1, 1972 a 122mm rocket hit between
the two barracks on this page.

A GI was wounded while in bed on the top
floor of this barracks at Bien Hoa Aug. 1, '72

Bien Hoa Airmen's Club destroyed in attack on
August 1, 1972 a few blocks from my barracks.

An A-37 Dragonfly nearly destroyed in attack
on Bien Hoa August 1, 1972.

A-37 Dragonfly loaded with bombs, ready for a
mission at Bien Hoa Air Base before attack.

The same plane after being blown up in attack
on August 1, 1972. 122mm rocket did this.

This building housed the Airlift Control
Center and message center in October 1971
when this picture was taken.

The same building after attack on August 1,
1972. It was the Base Operations Office and
the Transient Alert Office then. Windows out.

Piece of 122mm rocket sticking out of a hole
near aircraft revetment at Bien Hoa Aug.1,'72.

Piece of 122mm Russian-made rocket. CCCP can
be seen on it. A friend found it and gave it
to me for a souvineer August 1, 1972.

CHAPTER SIX

MARCH 1972

The first week in March 1972, eight members of my detachment got orders transferring them to other bases in Vietnam to finish out their tours. Apparently, other 8th Aerial Port detachments were short-handed because of the Vietnamization draw-down and since our workload at Bien Hoa had decreased in comparison to what it had been last year, we lost eight more members of our dwindling workforce.

Three of the guys leaving were currently assigned to Tri-Service ATCO. That meant I'd probably be working a 12-hour shift there again, starting soon because we wouldn't have enough people to work an 8-hour shift anymore.

If I didn't have orders at CBPO for me to go to Clark Air Base, Philippines, I'd stand a good chance of being re-assigned in-country too. I just couldn't understand why they didn't give me those orders yet. What were they waiting for? It made me feel very uncertain about my future.

During the Vietnam War, GIs not only sent letters home when they could but voice tapes as well. Cassette tapes were used to personalize the mail and many GIs received voice tapes from their friends and loved ones. That's why so many GIs owned cassette tape players, mostly small portable battery-operated ones they could carry around with them.

I bought a used one from another guy in the barracks and used it a few times. I recorded most of the Bob Hope USO show and also a friend of mine one night when an attack on the base just happened coincidentally while I was recording.

One day I decided to make a voice recording of myself and send it to my parents. I played it back before I mailed it to them and I was surprised at how deep my voice sounded.

I almost didn't recognize my own voice because what I heard when I was talking didn't
sound the same to me as the voice that I recorded and played back on tape.

At this time,holders of Airmen's Club membership cards were allowed into the NCO Club.
I think it was because they had fewer customers now than before and there was a plan to
close down the Airmen's Club and consolidate
all clubs into one to hold down operating
costs.

In any case, I went to the NCO Club one
night with my roommates to have a drink and
enjoy the music from a live band. I'd never
seen nor heard an all-Korean band before, nor
had I ever heard of a band made up mostly of
women. They were unique in another way too.
After every couple of songs, they'd take a
break and then come back on stage wearing a
different outfit and they danced a lot too.
There was only one guy in this band. They
were really good and I took some pictures of
them in each of their different outfits.

I talked to some of the American civilians
at Bien Hoa who worked for Flying Tigers Airlines one day. I had no plans at the time to
stay in the Air Force beyond my four year enlistment. Since I liked my job and there
were similar jobs with civilian airline com-
panies, I wanted to talk to people who were
currently employed with an airline company
and see what I could learn from them. They
told me that they made more money working in
Vietnam than they would have made back in the
states. The bad news was, with U.S. forces
leaving Vietnam for good, all of the airlines
that contracted with the Department of Defense
to transport troops and cargo would be laying
off a lot of people because of the loss of
that big contract. They told me that I might
get lucky and find a job with an airlines at a

major airport like the one in Atlanta. They
also suggested that I have a back-up plan in
case I didn't get hired. That's why I
thought about teaching.

It seemed like now that it was the month
of March, more and more rumors were going
around compared to previous months. I tried
to ignore them but some of them proved to be
true and then I got bit by the "rumor bug"
and shared the rumors with my friends. The
most talked about rumor was that a lot of us
were going to be leaving here long before our
normal DEROS (Date Estimated Return from
Overseas).

My barracks and others as well had more
empty rooms now than ever before. The second
floor had already been totally cleaned out
and boarded up a long time ago. My roommates
and I were already discussing the possibility
of everyone having their own private room to
ourselves. It was just a matter of time.

On our next day off, we played basketball
at the gym and then went for a swim in the
pool that was built right next to it. The
pool was a relaxing place to discuss all the
changes going on and speculate about our futures. There was much to speculate about.

One day in March I was walking from the
chow hall back to the barracks. A Chief Master Sergeant (E-9) stopped me to talk. He
noticed the West Georgia College logo on my
T-shirt and asked me where I was from. He
also asked me my name and Dad's name and then
said that he knew him when they were both
stationed at Dobbins Air Force Base in
Marietta, Georgia in the late 1950s. What a
coincidence!

Not long after that I met an Air Force
Captain who went to Valdosta State College in
Georgia. We talked about our two colleges
being tied in basketball that year. Again,
it was a case of someone seeing the West

Georgia College logo on my T-shirt.

I took another bus ride over to Long Binh Army Base to get my stereo back from their repair shop. It seemed like forever since I took it there to get fixed. They had to order a new fuse and a transistor because my roommate crossed some wires when he was connecting a fifth speaker to it. He repaid me for the repair bill.

Once again I got selected for guard duty. They gave me the 7 - 10 p.m. shift in the freight yard. It wouldn't have been so bad had it not been my night off. Also, they provided me with a flashlight to defend myself with, instead of a gun. My instructions were to "check the freight yard every few minutes and don't let anyone steal anything." There was a war going on, the VC had already snuck onto the base and blown stuff up and all they gave me was a flashlight, again! It's a miracle that more GIs didn't get killed here, including me!

My two roommates were both gone on leave for two weeks in March so I had the rooms all to myself. I wasn't used to this much quiet.

Around the middle of March I found out when I was leaving Vietnam, sort of. Somebody in my detachment found out from a friend of theirs who worked in CBPO and who saw the orders before the orders went to our commander for distribution to each of us. The special orders with 40 people on them were dated March 20, 1972 and changed our DEROS to April 5, 1972. There was only one catch. "Actual departure date will be determined by Unit Commander" was printed on Special Order P-98. That meant our departure from Bien Hoa may or may not be on that particular day.

We didn't have any more direct flights to Clark Air Base, Philippines from here so I'd

have to go to Tan Son Nhut Air Base in Saigon
to get a flight there. So the rumor about a
lot of us leaving much sooner than our normal
DEROS had been true after all! That still
left a few other rumors floating around.

About this time, someone showed me a form
letter that I found to be very amusing. You
just inserted your own name in the blank
space that was provided for a name and then
you sent it to your friends and family. I
typed a copy of it and after finding out that
I might be leaving here soon, sent it to my
family. The following is word-for-word and
with the exact spelling and punctuation, that
letter:

DEAR FRIENDS AND RELATIVES,
     In the very near future, the under-
signed, Steve Crews, will once again be
in your presence, dehydrated and demoral-
ized, to take a place again as a human
being, with the well-known form of Freedom and Justice for all; to engage in the
life, liberty, and the somewhat delayed
persuit of happiness.
     In making your joyous preparations to
welcome him back into organized society,
you shall need to provide certain allowances for the crude environment which has
been his miserable lot for the past
eleven months. In other words, he might
be a little Asiatic from Vietnamization
and should be handled with care. DO NOT
be alarmed if he is infected with eleven
types of rare tropical diseases. A little
time in "THE LAND OF THE FREE" will cure
his madness. Therefore, show no alarm if
he insists on carrying a weapon to the
dinner table, looks for his steel pot when
offered a chair, or wakes up in the middle
of the night for guard duty. Keep cool
when he pours gravy on his desert or mixes

milk with his peaches. Pretend not to
notice if he eats with his fingers instead of silverware and prefers C-rations to steak and take it with a smile
when he insists on digging up the gar-
den to fill sandbags for the bunker he's
building. Be tolerent when he takes
his blankets and sheets off his bed and
puts them on the floor to sleep.

Refrain from saying anything about
powdered eggs, de-hydrated potatoes,
roast beef, cool aid, or ice cream. Do
not be alarmed if he should jump up from
the dinner table and rush to a garbage
can to wash his dishes with a toilet
brush, after all, this has been his
standard; also if it should start to
rain, pay no attention to him if he
pulls off his clothes, grabs a bar of
soap and towel and rushes outside to
take a shower.

NEVER ask why the Jones' son held a
higher rank than he and by no means mention the term "RE-UP." Pretend not to
notice, if at a restaurant, he calls
the waitress a "Number One Girl" and
uses his hat for an ashtray. He will
probably keep listening for "Coming Home
Soldier" by Bobby Vinton on AFVN (Armed
Forces Vietnam) Radio; if he does, comfort him, for he is still reminissing.
Be especially watchful when he is in the
presence of women...ESPECIALLY beautiful
women!!!

Above all, keep in mind that beneath
this tanned and rugged exterior lies a
heart of gold, (THE ONLY THING OF VALUE
HE HAS LEFT). Treat him with kindness
and an occasional glass of good wine,
and you'll be able to rehabilitate that
which was once the happy-go-lucky guy
you once knew and loved. LAST BUT NOT
LEAST...

Send no more mail to this APO, fill
the refrigerator with plenty of ice,
and something cool to drink; get the
civies out of the moth balls, fill the
car with gas, and get the women and
children off the streets...
CAUSE THE KID IS COMING HOME!!!

This form letter was more relevant to
someone in the Army or Marine Corps who
spent a lot of time out in the field than an
Air Force airman who was on a large base all
the time. Still, I saw the humor in it and a
connection to some of it. I remember in
basic training when we actually did wash our
plates in a garbage can with a toilet brush.
One plastic-lined garbage can had hot soapy
water in it and the one next to it was full
of clear water for rinsing. The toilet brush
had never been used in a toilet. The long
handle and brush design made it perfect for
being used as a scrubbing tool for metal
plates.

Now that the Vietnamese holiday of Tet was
over, we were told that Saigon was not going
to be off limits to GIs any more. After my
roommates got back from their leave, I was
planning on asking for a 3-day pass in place
of an R & R and visit Saigon.
I went to the swimming pool again and just
by coincidence a friend of mine that was also
going to Clark Air Base was there too. He
was swimming on his back and he showed me how
to do it. I caught on pretty quick and was
swimming from one side of the pool to the
other in no time. I could also swim with my
face under water with a good over-the-head
stroke but I still swam like I was in a race,
unable to relax in the water. I was having
so much fun that I didn't realize that I was
getting sunburned again until the next day.
When would I ever learn?

I went to the movie theater sometime during the third week of March and saw The
Reivers. That week I also got permission to
go to Saigon from March 23rd to the 25th on a
3-day pass. I thought it might be my last
chance to do some sight-seeing since there
was a good chance I'd be out of the country
in another couple of weeks.

Most of the flights I helped process in
March were either C-130 in-country flights or
flights that brought few people in from the
states but went out full or almost full of
GIs that completed their tours and were getting on that big beautiful "Freedom Bird" going back to "The World." Some days we had a
few planes to work, other days were extra
busy.

My roommates got back from their two week
leave. They spent a couple of days telling
me all about their trip, their adventures and
what it was like back in the USA. They
really had a good time, except for a few travel delays. They were really surprised to
find out that my DEROS had been changed from
October 1972 to April 5, 1972 but theirs had
not. They got here when I did, so we spent
some time speculating what would happen to
them. Some of the 40 people on the new orders were being transferred to Tan Son Nhut
Air Base to complete a full year in-country
there instead of being sent to a stateside
base. I still had no assignment orders so I
was still wondering if that would happen to
me too and if I'd leave on April 5th or
later. The suspense was driving us crazy.

When I was in Vietnam, a lot of guys had a
"short-timer" calendar. It was a calendar in
which they used to keep track of how much
time they had left on their tours. Their
first day in-country left them with 364 more
days to go, unless they were Marines. They
did a 13-month tour instead of the standard

12-month tour all the other services did.
When a person had less than 100 days to go,
they became a "double-digit midget." Your
last day in Vietnam was known as a "wake up."
So, if you were leaving Vietnam four days
from today, you'd say, "Short! Three days
and a wake-up!" The word "short" was slang
for the term "short-timer," meaning someone
who only had a short time to go to finish
their tour. One favorite saying of short-
timers was, "I'm so short, I can't see over
the top of my boots!" With the possibility
of leaving Vietnam as early as April 5, 1972,
I started to feel like a "double-digit midget." Short!!!

I had talked to my first supervisor about
going to Saigon. He told me about a place
called the Kangaroo Club and how to find it.
He said that they knew him there and that if
I told the people there that I was a friend
of his, they would treat me right.
I started my 3-day pass with a long bus
ride. The big green Army bus left Bien Hoa
Air Base and stopped at the 1st Cav gate between Bien Hoa and the Navy's Seabee compound. Then it stopped at the entrance to
the Seabee compound a short ways down the
same road. From there we went to USARV HQ
(U.S. Army Republic of Vietnam Headquarters)
on Long Binh Army Base. The next (and final)
stop was at MACV HQ (Military Assistance
Command Vietnam Headquarters) in Saigon,
across the street from Tan Son Nhut Air Base.
Sometimes the bus would make a stop before
reaching MACV HQ. There was a place near one
of the bridges that crossed the Saigon River
where some Americans worked. There were lots
of large cargo ships docked there and I think
the place was called Newport. I went inside
of that place by the docks on one of my trips
by bus to Saigon.
There was lots of bumper-to-bumper traffic

from the outskirts of Saigon's northeast
side where the bus came in from Long Binh to
the northwest side where MACV HQ was. Luckily it was an uneventful trip and I was glad
because I rode "shotgun."

After everyone was seated on the bus at
Bien Hoa, a guy got on the bus with a couple
of guns. I was sitting in one of the front
seats and I was handed an M-16 rifle and a
bandolier full of clips. The guy across the
aisle from me was given a holstered .45 cal-
iber semi-automatic pistol. It was the model
1911 that the Army was still using. He also
was given a bandolier full of clips. We were
instructed to shoot anyone who tried to get
on or stop the bus in between the regular
stops. How ironic, I thought. I stand on
guard duty at night with only a flashlight
but now I'm riding a bus during the day and I
get a fully-loaded M-16 assault rifle with a
bandolier full of clips. I'll take this over
a flashlight any day!

That reminded me of the old Western movies
where one guy drives the stagecoach full of
passengers and the guy next to him holds a
shotgun to defend them from robbers and In-
dians. That's where the term "riding shotgun" came from. Now I was "riding shotgun"
in Vietnam for real with the possibility of
having to use a weapon.

Was I nervous? You better believe it! I
kept looking out the windows for anyone that
looked suspicious and tried to look into
other vehicles that got near us, looking for
anyone who had a weapon. We were met at MACV
HQ by someone who collected our guns and ammo
from us. I was very relieved that nothing
happened on the trip.

The next time I rode on that shuttle bus,
I sat all the way in the back. And wouldn't
you know it, there was a bullet hole an inch
or two over my window near where the side of
the bus starts curving towards the roof.

I rode in a taxi from MACV HQ to the President Hotel in downtown Saigon. It was a huge, heavily populated city and spread out for miles. I don't know which part of Saigon the hotel was in. I just remember that it was in a nice part of the city with wide streets and other large buildings next to it and large trees lined the street it was on. The first thing I noticed about it were the sandbagged guard posts on either side of the front door, with Vietnamese military police manning the positions. The hotel was 14 stories tall and was used mostly by American GIs who were either billeted there or stayed there while visiting Saigon like I was, on a 3-day pass.

I was given a room on the 12th floor. I left my clothes I'd brought along in the room and headed back downstairs to get a taxi. I went to the Kangaroo Club for awhile and then went to find a place to exchange some MPC (Military Payment Certificates) for some Vietnamese Piasters.

As I was walking along a sidewalk down the main street that the club was on, a young Vietnamese man who spoke English asked me what I was looking for. I told him I was looking for a money exchange place. He told me that on a nearby street there was a guy who gave the best exchange rate in the city, higher than the legal exchange rate. I went with him to a nearby street that was nothing more than an alley with shops down both sides and lots of people walking around. He introduced me to the guy and he asked me how much money I wanted to change. I don't remember the amount, maybe ten dollars worth of MPC. I watched as he counted out the Piasters, rolled them up tight and put a rubber band around the wad of bills. I think the rate then was about 425 Piasters to one MPC, so if you exchanged ten dollars MPC, you ended up with a big wad of Piasters.

Just as the money changer was about to put

the rolled-up wad of Piasters in my hand, he
said, "Make sure there aren't any police
watching." I turned my head to look at the
entrance to the alley for a second. In that
second, he switched the roll of Piasters with
another roll I didn't see he had hidden in
his other hand.

As soon as he got the MPC from me and gave
me the roll of Piasters, the two guys left in
a hurry. I just figured that they were not
legal money changers and were afraid of being
caught by the police. The bill on the outside of the roll in my hand was the same de-
nomination as on the first roll he'd shown me
before making the switch. I kept the roll of
Piasters in my front pocket until I got back
inside the Kangaroo Club. When I took the
roll out and removed the rubber band to count
out the total and pay for a drink I'd just
ordered, I quickly realized that I'd been
cheated. Instead of ten dollars worth of
Piasters, I had about two dollars worth.

That was a valuable lesson in how NOT to
make a money exchange. Now I didn't have
enough money to stay and have a good time.
Besides, I was so mad about being taken advantage of that I wasn't in the mood for a
good time either. I got another taxi and
went back to the President Hotel. Day one of
my three-day pass wasn't getting off to the
good start I'd hoped for. At least I still
had Friday and Saturday to look around and I
didn't have to be back at Bien Hoa until Sunday afternoon.

I ate supper in the hotel restaurant on
the 13th floor and then went to the large
game room, also on the same floor. I wanted
to shoot a few games of pool. There were
lots of women in the large game room, most of
whom were playing pool against other women.
There were only a couple of other American
men in there besides myself.

I found out that the women shooting pool

worked here. They were "hostesses," their job
being to entertain the guests. Waiters, wait-
resses and bell hops worked for tips to supp-
lement their low wages and so did the hostesses. Just like at the Apollo Club at Bien Hoa,
if you bought a hostess a drink, called a
"ladies drink" or "Saigon tea," it cost more
than your own and the hostesses got a cut of
the profits from their drinks. They were very
good at shooting pool and some of them made
extra money by betting on games.

One of the hostesses saw me eyeing the pool
tables and the other hostesses as well and
asked me if I'd like to play a game of pool.
She introduced herself as Lin (name changed to
protect her identity). I asked her what her
Vietnamese name was because I remembered the
girls in the Apollo Club used American-sound-
ing names and I thought that was what the
girls here did too. I was right. Her real
name was something totally different. She
told me that in Vietnam, people put their family name first and their first names last.
She pronounced her Vietnamese name for me but
preferred that I call her by her nickname Lin.

We talked about different things as we
played a game of pool and most of our talk was
about eachother's lives. She told me that she
was 23 years old and was a secretary for a
business machine company. She came here to
earn some extra money on her days off from her
regular job. She spoke English and French
fluently, having learned both in school.

As we talked and played pool, she noticed
me looking at another woman at a nearby table.
The woman didn't look Vietnamese to me but not
entirely Caucasian either. She was wearing a
mini-skirt which revealed a lot whenever she
had to bend over and stretch out to make a
difficult shot. I just couldn't resist looking. I wasn't used to seeing women as pretty
as her.

Lin asked me if I'd rather shoot pool with

the woman she'd seen me looking at. She said
it was OK with her if I did. Just to be polite, I said no and told her I was just looking at her out of curiosity because she did-
n't look Vietnamese to me. Lin told me the
woman's name and said that she was half-
French and half-Vietnamese. The French half
was clearly the predominant half. My mind
was saying, "Ooh la la, mon dieu! Oui, more
French for sure!" She was so much more good
looking than the 100% Vietnamese women here.
Lin was, in my opinion, the best looking
woman in the room except for "Frenchy," my
personal nickname for the woman I'd been
looking at. That's my story and I'm sticking
to it!

The President Hotel was a nice change of
sceenery for me in many ways. The next day,
Lin took me up to the 14th floor which was
the top of the building. It had a fence
around the edges so people couldn't fall or
jump from way up there. It was one of the
tallest buildings in the city. The view of
the surrounding countryside was amazing. The
land in that part of South Vietnam was flat
and I could see for miles in every direction.
I saw no signs of a war being fought, heard
no gunfire or explosions, and felt completely
safe.

On the top of this hotel were gardens with
ponds, water fountains, statues and real
grass, even park benches too. It was just
amazing and something I never expected to see
on top of a building. I'd brought my new instamatic camera with me and took some pictures of Lin sitting on a park bench. She
took some pictures of me with the pond and a
statue in the background. It was so casual,
so relaxing, and so hard to think that there
were people fighting and dying in a war in
this country that was so beautiful. It was
March 25, 1972 and things were about to
change in a big way. My life would never be

the same.

Lin and I talked for hours on end and she taught me a great deal about her life, Vietnamese customs, and how to avoid being taken advantage of, like in the money-changing scam that I'd experienced. She also taught me about life in other ways too and, just like in a few old World War II movies I'd seen where the American GI falls in love with a woman from England or France in a short period of time, I fell in love with her. I think those cases are referred to as "wartime romances." Now I was beginning to understand why it happened in the movies; because it happened in real life too, not just in the minds of movie producers in Hollywood.

Just before leaving New Jersey for Vietnam, my Grandpa Smith told me, "You better not come home married to a gook!" He was the Archie Bunker of the family as far as I was concerned. That's the kind of stuff I'd have to deal with if I did get married to a woman from an Asian country. Koreans, Vietnamese, it didn't matter. To some people, they were all "gooks."

Before my time was up in Saigon, Lin took me to her house in Cholon, the district of Saigon that was the equivalent of San Francisco's Chinatown. Lots of Chinese lived there. It took a long time to get there from the hotel. I was amazed at how big and spread out Saigon was.

Her house was a small wooden structure with a tin roof, located near a main road but in a narrow alley. There was one room downstairs and one upstairs. She slept on a traditional Vietnamese bed on the ground floor. It was all wood except for a woven mat placed over the wooden bed slats so you wouldn't get splinters in your rear end. Years later in the Philippines, I'd see the same type of bed used by the poor in that country too.

The room upstairs was only used for drying

clothes on a line strung from one wall to
the other. That room was too hot for anything else. The ground floor room also had
an electric fan, a few pots and pans kept in
a cabinet and a few pictures, candles and
personal things. There was also a "night
pot," as she called it. A hundred and fifty
years ago in America, every home had a
"chamber pot" which served as a human waste
collector before indoor plumbing, and that
was what she had.

There was a communal bathroom down the
street but she told me it smelled really bad
and was very dirty. It was used by many
others on a first-come-first-serve basis.
There was no indoor plumbing of any kind in
her house. She had a large plastic container to catch rainwater in, to use for bathing
and washing clothes and dishes. This was a
primitive way to live compared to anything I
had ever seen before.

Life for her and hundreds of thousands of
other Vietnamese was getting harder with
each passing year. Inflation was at an all-
time high. The black marketing of American-
made goods had a lot to do with it. Some
local stores sold everything from beer and
liquor from U.S. military Class VI stores
and Brand-name ciggerettes, C-rations, uniforms, even weapons and ammo, all from the
USA. With thousands of Americans leaving
Vietnam each month and facilities being
turned over to the South Vietnamese government or shut down forever like the Marine
base at Khe Sanh, tens of thousands of Vietnamese were out of a job every month because they had been working for the Americans that left. Laundry workers, office
workers, cooks and kitchen help, garbage
collectors, NCO and Officer's Club employees
and entertainers along with others who helped keep the bases running with water, electricity, carpenters, plumbers, you name it.

The situation was bad and getting worse daily.
     Even the Mama-sans at Bien Hoa who did our
laundry and made our beds had less than half
the customers they used to have when I got
there in October. They were now making less
than half of the earnings they used to make.
Try taking a 50%-60% pay cut and see how you
live on a lot less. It really made me appreciate what I had and the country I'd lived in
before coming here.
     When it was time for me to check out of the
hotel and head back to Bien Hoa, I told Lin
that I'd come back and visit her again every
chance I got. She didn't believe me, thinking
that every GI said the same thing, kind of
like when a date ends and the girl tells the
guy, "Call me" and gives him her number but
even though he says he will, he never does. I
wasn't like that.

     When I got back to Bien Hoa, I had some
mail waiting for me. Something in one of my
mother's letters set me off. Some things had
to do with photos I'd sent home of the Korean
almost-all girl band wearing skimpy clothing.
I don't remember what else in the letter got
me upset. I normally wrote short letters
home but the next one I wrote ended up being
a record for me, eleven pages long. One of
the things I mentioned was that I was in love
with Lin. I just knew that my parents would
be shocked after they got that news.
     In the very next letter I wrote home, I
apologized for things I'd written in the previous one. It took me over fourteen hours to
finish the four page letter because of so
many interruptions.

CHAPTER SEVEN

APRIL 1972

In February 1972, President Nixon went to
China to talk to Mao Tse-tung. He wanted to
re-establish diplomatic relations with the
Communist Chinese. The Chinese had sent
military advisors and weapons to help North
Vietnam. The North Vietnamese had been
stockpiling weapons for awhile and they were
ready for another big attack against South
Vietnam. We read about Nixon's visit to
China in the newspaper and had no idea about
North Vietnam's plans and no idea why our
president would want to be friendly towards
one of our enemies.

On Tuesday April 4, 1972, North Vietnamese
troops began a three-pronged attack against
South Vietnam. It's estimated that over
200,000 North Vietnamese attacked Quang Tri
in the northern part of South Vietnam, Kontum
in the central part of the country and An Loc
in the south. The enemy first crossed the
Demilitarized Zone and attacked Quang Tri
which was the nearest large city to it. A
few days later they attacked Kontum and on
April 13th, they attacked An Loc. Because
these attacks happened around Easter, they
became known as the Easter Offensive. It
lasted from April 4 to October 22, 1972 and I
was there the entire time. When the attacks
began, only 69,000 U.S. military personnel
were in South Vietnam and very few of those
were combat troops.

An Loc was the capital of Binh Long pro-
vince. It was northwest of Bien Hoa and
Saigon. During the battle for An Loc, aircraft flying from Tan Son Nhut and Bien Hoa
gave the South Vietnamese troops and their
American military advisors the fighter-
bomber support they needed. An Loc was
surrounded by the enemy for awhile and land

resupply became impossible. C-130s flying
from their home bases of Clark Air Base,
Philippines, Ching Chuan Kang Air Base,
Taiwan and from bases in Thailand were used to
air-drop supplies into surrounded An Loc. The
first airlift resupply missions by American
aircraft were flown on April 15, 1972. Some
of the C-130s landed at Bien Hoa and many of
the Vietnamese Air Force A-1 Skyraiders and
F-5 Freedom Fighters stationed at Bien Hoa
took part in the battle for An Loc. The Bien
Hoa flightline became busier than ever and
presented me with more aircraft photo opportunities.

During the Easter Offensive, while American
troop strength in South Vietnam continued to
decline, the activities of the U.S. Air Force
increased. Bombing missions increased and resupply missions did as well. We found ourselves working harder with fewer people. Our
government replaced the tanks and artillery
pieces and aircraft that the South Vietnamese
lost in combat and supplied them with more
ammunition and military supplies. A lot of
that stuff came through Bien Hoa but a lot
more was delivered to Tan Son Nhut and they
needed more people there to help load and unload aircraft.

On April 7, 1972 Bien Hoa was attacked
again. Three or four 122mm rockets hit that
Thursday at 0100 in the morning. Some of my
friends were at work outside of the terminal
building and the rockets hit close enough for
them to see them explode. They did some damage to some buildings and equipment but no
Americans were killed or injured. I was in
Saigon at the time, visiting Lin and proving
to her that I meant it when I told her that
I'd visit her every chance I got. I think it
made a big impression on her and a very positive one too.

During that visit, we talked about a lot of

things, including getting married. On that
trip, I saw a lot of tanks and APCs (armored
personnel carriers) heading north out of
Saigon. Lin had a brother in the ARVN (Army
of the Republic of Vietnam) stationed up
north in Quang Tri where the first big
battles of the Easter Offensive took place.

I later went to the base legal office at
Bien Hoa to find out about all that was required to get married in Vietnam. Then I
talked to my first sergeant and then the
Catholic chaplain. They both advised
against it plus the two countries had so
many requirements to be met that they tried
to make it hard for American servicemen to
marry Vietnamese nationals.

On April 14, 1972 I was working at night
when Tan Son Nhut Air Base in Saigon got hit
by one rocket. It didn't cause any injuries.
Another rocket hit a marketplace near the
base and killed 12 innocent civilians and
wounded another four. I heard about that
attack on the radio. As far as I knew, that
was the second attack against Tan Son Nhut
since I'd gotten here last October.

At work that day, we were told that, because of increasing attacks in the area, nobody would be leaving our base for any re-
assignments, even if their year-long tour was
over. So I figured that I would not be going to Clark Air Base any time soon.

April 15th was supposed to be my day off
but it got so busy with extra cargo and passenger flights that someone was sent to the
barracks to get me to come to work and help
out.

At 3a.m. April 16th, I got a break to get
something to eat. The snack bar next to the
terminal was closed and the chow hall was
too far to walk to so I walked to my barracks.
I always had some kind of food or snacks to
eat there. I saw that someone tried to break

into my room. The screws in the hinges and
latch were loose and the big metal part of the
latch was all bent out of shape. Nothing was
missing so I guess they gave up trying to get
in. Three other guys on the night shift had
their doors messed up too so we figured that
it had to have been done by someone who knew
our work schedule, someone in our own unit.

We all went to the first sergeant and reported it to him first. Then we all went to
the MPs (military police) and made signed
statements. The weird thing was, nobody had
anything missing, just damaged doors. I
changed the lock and removed the screws from
the door and latch and replaced them with
real long nails that were hammered flat on the
other side of the door.

By the middle of April 1972, Bien Hoa Air
Base was receiving lots of transiting F-4
Phantoms and A-4 Skyhawk jet fighter-bombers.
Whenever an F-4 took off at night, it made
quite a sight and sound. They were very loud
when they turned on their afterburners as they
released their brakes and began their takeoff
roll. The best part of watching them take
off for me was when long pink jets of flame
shot out behind both engines as they roared
down the runway. The long tail of pink flames
only went out after they turned off their
afterburners. By that time they were high in
the air and on their way to reign death and
destruction down on the enemy.

We also started seeing more old C-119 Flying Boxcars belonging to the Vietnamese Air
Force landing here. They were used by our Air
Force in the Korean War. We knew that the
battle for An Loc was the reason we were getting more planes in, some types not having been
seen landing here before. That included Navy
and Marine Corps aircraft too, not just U.S.
Air Force F-4s.

Aircraft mechanics and cooks from other

bases were coming to Bien Hoa now on TDY
(temporary duty) status. With all the extra
planes landing here, some needed maintenance
work and their crews needed to be fed at all
hours of the day and night.

Our extra details and work schedules got
worse in April. Instead of having guard
duty in our freight yard one night a week,
we now had it five nights in a row, from 7
p.m.-1 a.m. Someone else took over at 1a.m.

They also cancelled all leaves, R & Rs and
3-day passes. That went on for awhile. The
only place we could travel to was Tan Son
Nhut by plane. There was no more shuttle bus
service.

We were also now required to have three
people in our office during the entire 12-
hour shift, regardless of whether or not
there was any work to do. Sleeping wasn't
allowed in the office either. We had a new
first sergeant, a new commander and a new
attitude towards this place and it wasn't a
positive one either.

On April 22nd I got to go to Saigon,
again on the shuttle bus that was run by the
Army. It seemed that one day we'd be told
one thing and the very next day be told something totally different, like not getting to
leave the base. I asked for a pass and got
one, with no problem at all. For the second
time this month, Bien Hoa got attacked during
my trip to Saigon. My friends were now telling me to let them know in advance when I was
going so they could prepare for the next
attack. What a coincidence!

I met Lin's father for the first time during this trip. It was a strange experience
for me because he performed a Buddhist good
luck ceremony for me. I felt like I was being knighted like they do in England with the
sword tap on the shoulders of the one being
knighted. I had to kneel down in front of

some type of indoor multi-tiered temple with
incense sticks lit and emitting a lot of smoke
with a statue of Buddha sitting behind all the
incense sticks. Lin's father tapped me on
each shoulder with a big sword and then gave
me a yellow cloth with Vietnamese writing on
it. He told me to keep the cloth in a safe
place and not to show it to anyone. Only Lin
and I could look at it, nobody else. Then he
folded the cloth neatly into a square and told
me I was now safe from harm. After he gave it
to me, I thanked him and was happy that the
ceremony was over. That big sword made me
nervous, especially when it was moving inches
away from my neck, going from one shoulder to
the other. I felt sure that few Americans
ever experienced something like that. He did
not speak any English, so Lin interpreted his
words for me.

I learned that he had once lived in Hue.
In 1968 during the Tet Offensive, his house
was destroyed in the battle for that city. He
moved to Saigon and bought his present home
for about $2,000.00 in Piasters. That was a
lot of money in this country at the time.

After visiting him, Lin and I went out to
eat at a Chinese restaurant in Cholon. I
tried to eat with chopsticks but failed. I
was glad they had forks for us foreigners.
Our meal was a real bargain. For 1,400 Piasters (about $3.50 in MPC), we had chicken and
rice with fried eggs chopped up in it, pork
fat strips, shrimp and mushrooms and pickled
crisp green beans and salad. Then we were
served hot tea and hot wash cloths for our
hands. That was something I'd never experienced before. The food was great and served
in such a large quantity that we could only
finish eating half of it.

I was the only American in the restaurant.
I was wearing civilian clothes but that didn't
make any difference as far as being the only
non-Asian in the place. For that matter, I

was the only non-Asian in the whole neighborhood as far as I could tell. I didn't feel
afraid for my safety at all. I should have,
but I didn't. Maybe there was something to
that Buddhist good luck charm after all.

CHAPTER EIGHT

MAY 1972

When I returned to Bien Hoa from my latest trip to Saigon, things were changing quickly. On Tuesday May 2nd, eight of us in the Passenger Service offices of the terminal were told we'd be going to work at Tan Son Nhut Air Base for a 29-day TDY. The first sergeant said the TDY would probably be changed to PCS (permanent change of station) and that we should take everything we owned with us. Where had I heard this before? Every week we got a new story. I actually hoped that it would be true this time because my former supervisor was now on his second tour of duty, this time at Tan Son Nhut. He'd recently told a friend of mine that they were short-handed there and that if I put in for a transfer, it might get approved.

I had already tried that and was turned down. So this was going to work out to my benefit after all. Plus, it would lessen the amount of traveling I had to do to visit Lin.

On May 3rd I was on a bus with everything I owned, which wasn't very much. Along with me was A1C Francis Barner, A1C Patrick Baugh, one of my roommates, A1C Armand Fecteau, A1C Alvin Howard, A1C James Miller, A1C Christopher Montero, and A1C William Newborg. The first sergeant told us that we were on verbal orders for now and that regular TDY orders would be given to us in the near future. The orders weren't given to us until July! They were dated 1 July 1972 and said we were authorized travel by military aircraft, even though we went by bus. The purpose of the TDY, according to our orders was: "To augment 8APS Air Freight and Traffic Control sections." There was no mention of Passenger Service, which is all most of us knew, had been trained for, and had experience in. We were in for a big dose of OJT (on-the-job training). Personally, I

was very disappointed. I wanted to stay in
a Passenger Service job.

After arriving at Tan Son Nhut Air Base,
we were shown to our barracks so we could
put all of our belongings away. On the outside, they looked similar to our barracks at
Bien Hoa except that these weren't built in
the shape of an H. Our rooms here were less
than half the size of the ones we had at
Bien Hoa. There was a bunkbed and two gray
metal wall lockers in each room and no space
for anything else. There was a thin plywood
wall between the hallway and each room.
There were no walls separating individual
rooms, only wall lockers set back-to-back.
The door of my room wasn't even on hinges.
It leaned against the frame and a cheap
hasp, which you could put a lock on, kept it
from falling over.

The barracks had no latrine nor a water
fountain. You had to walk three buildings
down the row of barracks to get to the building which was one huge latrine and nothing
else. Pity the poor soul that was sick with
diarrhea and had to go find a toilet in a
hurry and had to go three or more buildings
away to get there. I hated the place!

I was assigned to the Inbound Processing
section of Air Freight. This was where all
the cargo that got off-loaded from military
and civilian aircraft went before it got distributed to the organization it was intended
for. Because of the increase in flights here
and a manpower shortage, we were on 12-hour
shifts, working nine days straight before we
got one day off. I was on the 7 a.m. - 7 p.m.
shift.

One of the guys in my TDY group was assigned to an office where aircraft movement
records were made. He got to work indoors in
air conditioned comfort. The other six guys
in the group all got assigned to a section

called Line Loading. They basically became
pallet-pushers, loading cargo on some planes,
unloading cargo from others.

When I first started working in Inbound
Cargo Processing, they had me do simple tasks
like assisting others in removing cargo nets
and plastic pallet covers from cargo pallets.
There was a long line of metal rollers that
went from near the flightline side of a covered structure called the pole barn to the
other side of the pole barn where our section
was located. Most days the rollers had lines
of cargo pallets that had been recently taken
off of arriving aircraft.

The cargo pallets were moved to an open
space with three-point dunnage, using a 10K
forklift. The dunnage consisted of four foot
long pieces of 4" X 4" thick wood that were
spread apart evenly so the tines of the forklift could place the pallets down without letting them touch the ground.

The next step was to remove the cargo manifest that was inside of a plastic pouch and
stapled onto one of the cargo nets. We'd
then remove the top net and two side nets and
any tie-down straps that may have been added
to help stabilize the cargo from shifting
around. Then the plastic pallet cover was
removed. That kept everything on the pallet
dry. Then the cargo nets had to be hung up
on special racks so they could dry out if they
were wet and also to keep them from becoming
tangled. The plastic pallet covers were put
in a large storage box if they were still in
good condition to be used again.

Most of the time, one guy would hold the
cargo manifest and check off the items with a
pen as the other guy called out the 17-digit
code that was on a label on each item on the
cargo pallet. Sometimes when we were extra
busy or short of people, one person would do
it all, including moving the cargo after the
inventory was done. It was a very labor-

intensive process.

Once the items were accounted for, they would be moved to another part of the freight yard that contained pallets on 3-point dunnage. Next to each pallet was a sign that showed the unit that cargo was going to. For example, Base Supply had a sign that had FB5250 on it. Incoming cargo that had a matching code on the label would be placed on that pallet. Base Supply would send people over every day to pick up their stuff that was on their designated pallet.

I spent many hours each day out in the hot sun and high humidity moving cargo either by hand or forklift from the inventory area to the "ready-to-be-picked-up area." This process went on 24 hours a day, 7 days a week.

Whenever we received outsize cargo, things too large to put on a pallet like tanks and artillery pieces, that stuff was put in a separate area near the flightline. There were signs there too, designating the unit it was going to.

When I got off work and went to the barracks, I ran into an unexpected problem. There were no lights in the rooms! There were lights in the hallway only. I had to string up the Christmas tree lights I'd brought with me from Bien Hoa to be able to see anything. Since there was no water fountain in the barracks either, I bought some soft drinks to quench my thirst. I put my mosquito net up around the bottom bunk and turned on my fan to circulate the hot humid air. At least I had this small space to myself. I hung my helmet and flak jacket on one of the bedposts where I could get to them quickly if we got attacked.

The noise level in the barracks was high because of the poor construction and lack of solid walls between rooms. I wasn't getting enough sleep because of the noise. I also wasn't getting enough to eat. At work, we got only one meal break a day. I got a lunch break from noon to 1:30 p.m. The reason they gave us so much time was because the chow hall and BX were so far away from where we worked. The BX opened after we started work and by the time we were off, it was closed. That was the only place we could buy soap, shaving supplies and boot polish. We could get some food and soft drinks there too. Sometimes I'd get lucky and get a base taxi or a passing military vehicle would stop and give me a ride. This was a big base, much larger than Bien Hoa and some things were far apart. A taxi would take you anywhere on base for a flat fee, no matter the distance. The fare was only 50 Piasters, or "P" as we called them. That was about 12½¢ at the exchange rate then.

After a few days of living in the barracks and getting fed up with the noise and not getting enough sleep and having to walk three buildings away just to go to the bathroom, I decided to visit Lin and discuss this with her.

We went out to eat at a Korean restaurant. I had sweet and sour pork, kimchee (the fresh fermented spicy cabbage, not the pickled-in-a jar kind you find in American grocery stores), some kind of hot vegetable that looked like turnips but was hot like a pepper, and vegetable soup. Since I'd been eating only one meal a day on base, I was now making up for it.

We talked about renting an apartment near the base. She would do that while I was working and I could only hope for something better. I hoped that she would find us an air conditioned apartment. I didn't know if it was legal for me to live in Saigon but I knew a lot of guys did so I'd just do what many of them did.

I managed to get the day off on May 7th so I could return to Bien Hoa to get my mail. The postal worker that I talked to there told me they'd forward my mail to General Delivery at

the post office at Tan Son Nhut, but the post
office there wouldn't give me a P.O. box because I didn't have any orders. After ex-
plaining to them why I was there with no orders, they agreed to let me get my mail at
the General Delivery window. What a hassle!

It was around this time in May that I
started feeling bad. I developed a sore
throat and went to the dispensary. They did
a throat culture test for strep throat. I
got a cholera and a plague shot that day as
well. My test for strep throat came back
negative and that was a relief.

I told my friends who'd accompanied me on
this TDY from Bien Hoa what I'd seen at Bien
Hoa on my trip to get my mail. The work load
had gotten lighter there. The snack bar near
the passenger terminal had closed due to lack
of business as well as the Stars and Stripes
bookstore inside the terminal. The chow hall
was in the process of closing and moving to
the NCO Club. The base theater was even
closing in another week because of fewer
patrons.

Of course it wasn't only Air Force personnel leaving. Starting in May and continuing through June 1972, the 3rd Brigade of the
1st Cavalry Division (Airmobile) and the
196th Infantry Brigade departed Vietnam.

One day around this time I heard some guys
talking about our planes bombing North Vietnam and mining their harbors. I thought that
should have been done years ago when Johnson
was president. I liked President Nixon's
actions against North Vietnam.

Whenever I got to see the news on TV, they
showed anti-war demonstrators protesting
against the war. I wondered why they didn't
protest against the Communist North Vietnamese for invading South Vietnam. They
were the ones trying to take away another

country's freedom. It seemed to me that the
anti-war protestors didn't seem to care about
that issue at all. It bothered me a lot, especially when I just saw a couple of teenage
South Vietnamese soldiers who lost their
lower left legs and were walking around with
crutches. They'd given a lot trying to keep
their country free.

Lin and I went to the Saigon zoo on May
17th. I wore my tan uniform called 1505s.
We saw bears, elephants, tigers, etc. but one
thing this place had that no American zoo had
was a Buddhist temple, located near the entrance.

I finally got some mail on May 20th, after
not receiving any for three weeks. One
letter was postmarked May 11, another May 15
and a third had a May 16 postmark. That led
me to believe that mail was being held at
Bien Hoa because either they couldn't drive
the mail truck to Saigon because of road dangers or because I had no orders for them or
the post office at Tan Son Nhut to use as
authorization to forward it here.

The rainy season was starting early this
year. I'd been told that it began in June in
this part of the country. Unlike the United
States where we had Spring, Summer, Fall and
Winter, here there were only two seasons, dry
and rainy. I called them hot and dry and hot
and wet. As of May 21st, it had rained every
day for the past two weeks.

Whenever it rained at work, downpours happened only a few minutes after clouding up.
We had to stop whatever we were doing and put
plastic pallet covers over everything. We
got soaked in the process. Even if there was
lightning nearby, some of the NCOs told us to
keep covering stuff, regardless of the danger.

One day I got fed up with getting soaked
and risking my life by possibly getting hit

by lightning. When the rain came down so
hard that visibility was only a few feet and
nobody was near me, I got under a plastic
pallet cover and stood next to the cargo
that was stacked higher than my head. I was
able to stay relatively dry. I was already
wet some but at least the pounding rain was
no longer soaking me more. When the rain
stopped after about ten to fifteen minutes,
I went back to work again and nobody said
anything to me because I was out of view for
a few minutes. My point of view was, there
was no cargo here worth dying for and lightning could surely kill you.

Lieutenant Colonel Crutchfield was my
first commander at Bien Hoa. Now he was
back again as our Station Traffic Officer at
Tan Son Nhut. He was the second person I'd
known so far that got transferred from Bien
Hoa to Tan Son Nhut. I was unable to figure
out why they could do that but I couldn't.
Well, at least being here TDY helped me see
Lin more often.

She and I went to a movie in downtown
Saigon one day and it was next to a small
park. Coming attractions were normally
shown on colorful posters on the outside
walls of the theater. On this day, in place
of movie posters, there were many black and
white photos taken of a battle under the
glass in their place. Some of the photos
were pretty graphic, showing dead soldiers
on the ground and some stuck in barbed wire.
Most of them were North Vietnamese and a few
of them were blown to pieces. In the park
nearby were many enemy weapons on display.
The largest one was a PT-76 tank which was
first made in Russia in the early 1950s.
There were also machine guns of all types
and sizes and large crew-served anti-aircraft guns on display. That was the first

time I'd ever seen an RPG (rocket-propelled grenade) up close as well as the other weapons like AK-47s and SKS rifles.

I don't remember much about the movie we saw but I do remember French and English words that appeared at the bottom of the screen. If you couldn't understand the Vietnamese the actors spoke, you could follow the story by reading the words under the action.

Later that day, I was introduced to one of Lin's brother-in-laws. He was a QC (Quang Cong - Vietnamese Military Police). He'd been in that job for the last six years. He had five kids and got paid 12,000 Piasters a month. That was equal to $30.00, one dollar a day for a family of seven to live on. That was an average wage here, for a Vietnamese soldier. And I thought my pay was low!

Armed Forces Radio and Television Service had a broadcast station in Saigon. Now that I was closer to it than before, I got better reception on my little 5-inch black and white TV. In addition to the daily news, they showed programs that were popular back in the USA. Sometimes I was just too tired to watch TV at night and some shows came on too late for me to stay up and watch so I really didn't see much TV. Most evenings I just wanted to lay down and rest my weary body and go to sleep.

Lin and I rented an apartment that she'd found for us in May, about two weeks after my TDY to Tan Son Nhut started. We had one large room with a private bath on the third floor of a four-story apartment building. We had a queen size bed, a dresser and a chair. It was not air conditioned but it did have a ceiling fan which we ran continuously. The entrance to the apartment was on the outside part of the building at the end of a small balcony. It overlooked a narrow road with other apartment buildings on both sides of it.

Our apartment was only a few blocks away
from the Army's 3rd Field Hospital. I could
walk to the base gate across the street from
MACV Headquarters in about ten minutes.
Every morning I'd see lots of other American
GIs and civilians walking into the gate so I
knew that I wasn't the only guy with a room
in the barracks and a place in town.

I met several American civilians who lived
in my neighborhood that worked for Pacific
Architechs and Engineers (PA&E). We received
some cargo for that company just about every
day. Some of those guys lived with their
Vietnamese girlfriends and some were married
to Vietnamese as well. That made my situation seem more acceptable to me.

Lin bought food for us in a market and one
day brought home some fruit that I'd never
seen nor eaten before. I thought the papaya
was OK and the yellow mangos tasted great.
The thing I couldn't stand because of the
smell was the durian. It was larger than the
papaya and had little spikes all over the
outer dark green skin. As soon as she cut it
open to clean out the seeds, the smell hit me.
Wow, what a stink! She ate it and liked it.
Not me!

Because of the big battles going on during
the Communist Easter Offensive of 1972, more
aircraft flew in with more supplies to replace
a lot used and lost. We still needed more
help with the increased workload at Tan Son
Nhut. That's why two more guys from my detachment at Bien Hoa were sent here.

They got here the first part of the last
week in May. For five days they were assigned
to the Inbound Freight section to help get the
cargo offloaded from arriving aircraft. They
filled me in on what was going on back at Bien
Hoa. They said Marines now outnumbered Air
Force personnel because some A-4 Skyhawks they
flew had arrived from their base in Japan.

They brought along all of their aircraft
maintenance and weapons systems personnel and
their own cooks and cargo handling people as
well. They reopened many of the barracks
that had been empty and boarded up and took
over the passenger terminal too. There were
so many of them now at Bien Hoa that the chow
hall reopened and the movie theater did too.
The base went from being almost a ghost town
back to being the fully-staffed and busy base
it was when I'd first gotten there.
     Bien Hoa received another rocket attack at
10:30 p.m. May 23, 1972. Three 122mm
Russian-made rockets killed one Vietnamese
and wounded ten others. No Americans were
hit in the attack this time.

     Sometime during the last week of May 1972,
I took a ride in an M-48 medium tank, by
accident. A shipment of tanks, APCs and am-
phibious vehicles we called "Ducks" arrived
one day. We had no latrine in our work area
and I had to walk a long way to get to the
nearest one. The Inbound Cargo Processing
building I worked out of was a small wooden
two room affair with sandbags stacked up
waist high around it. On the way back from
the latrine that day, I decided to make a
small detour and check out the tanks parked
in the arrival area where all non-palletized
cargo was placed right after being off-loaded
from planes.
     I walked up to a tank, looked around to
see if anyone was looking in my direction,
and then climbed up on it quickly. The top
turret hatch was easy to open and I climbed
in and shut it after me. I looked around inside the main compartment and then looked in
the driver's compartment to my left, in the
front corner. Within a few seconds I heard
voices and then footsteps on the tank. I got
over to the other side of the main compartment, as far from the driver's seat as I

could because the hatch over the driver's
seat was opened by someone climbing in and I
didn't want anyone to see me inside there
where I didn't belong.

Within a few seconds of entering the tank,
whoever was sitting in the driver's seat,
started the engine. I froze in place, thinking about what I should do. I decided that
as soon as the driver exited the tank, I'd go
out the same way I got in. I didn't want to
get in any kind of trouble for not being
where I was supposed to be, which was at work.

The tank began moving and I had no idea
where it was going. I hoped that it would
stop soon so I could get out. When it finally stopped, a couple of minutes had passed
by so I thought we hadn't gone very far. The
driver turned the engine off and then got out
through his hatch. I could hear him walking
across the top of the tank, heading towards
the back. I looked out of the small slit of a
window that was just below the top hatch and
saw the driver standing on the back of the
tank with his back to me. He was waving his
arms at another tank, directing it to park
right behind this one. We were just outside
the perimeter fence of the air base, parked
along the road that ran between the base and
MACV Headquarters. In one direction was the
city of Saigon, in the other was wide open
countryside just a short distance from here.

My heart was pounding hard and fast as I
made my decision to get out then. I opened
the main hatch on top of the turret as quietly
as I could and got out of there so quietly and
quickly that the driver didn't notice me until
I was already on the ground walking past him,
headed for the gate we'd just driven out of a
moment ago. Out of the corner of my eye, I
could see him looking down at me with a surprised look on his face, as if he was thinking
to himself, "Where the devil did he just come
from?"

He and the other tank drivers were all
Vietnamese. As I walked back to my work area
I thought to myself, what if they were headed
to the battle going on at An Loc? I could
have ended up in big trouble. Upon my return
to Inbound Cargo Processing, one of the NCOs
asked me how I got over on one side of the
area when he'd seen me going to the latrine
in the opposite direction only a few minutes
ago. I don't remember what my response was,
but I didn't get in any trouble and that's
all I was concerned about.

The American made M-48 tank I had ridden
in had a crew of four. It had a top speed of
45 miles per hour. It was armed with one
76mm cannon and one 30 calibre machine gun.
It was flown here aboard an Air Force C-5A
Galaxy.

We gave the Vietnamese Army lots of them
because they lost many of them fighting
against the T-54 tanks used by the North
Vietnamese Army. The T-54 tank had a much
more powerful 100mm cannon. It was built in
Russia and was a heavy tank and the M-48 was
a medium tank and no match for the larger
one. A battle between these two tanks was
like David going up against Goliath. David
beat Goliath and the M-48 could possibly beat
a T-54, but only under certain circumstances.
Unfortunately for the South Vietnamese, those
circumstances did not happen often.

I was allowed to drive a forklift a little
more each day since a lot of cargo we received was too heavy to be lifted by hand. I
was taught how to do all the paperwork involved in the job and I was getting better at
both driving and doing paperwork. I was
supervised less and less as time went on.
That's how OJT (on-the-job training) is supposed to work.

TSgt (Technical Sergeant) Proctor was in
charge of my shift at the time and I thought

he was a very good NCO to work for. He
taught me a lot about air cargo work. Many
years later, I saw him again. I was an OT
(Officer Trainee) at the Air Force's Medina
Annex to Lackland Air Force Base. I'd finished a program called Operation Bootstrap
and was going through a 90-day program to
become a Second Lieutenant. I was in the
cafeteria when I spotted a table full of senior NCOs and one of them was Proctor, now a
Chief Master Sergeant (E-9).

I walked over to his table and introduced
myself and said something like, "I don't know
if you remember me or not but I worked for
you at Tan Son Nhut Air Base in 1972 in Inbound Processing for three months. I was TDY
from Bien Hoa and you wrote me a nice letter
of recommendation to take back with me, re-
commending that I get a 9 on my APR" (Airman
Proficiency Report, 9 being the highest rat-
ing you could get). I told him that the
letter of recommendation helped me get my
first APR recinded because of the manner in
which it was written and it opened up the
possibility of my acceptance to Officer
Training School. I thanked him and shook his
hand and told him that I never forgot what he
did for me and how I enjoyed working for him
in Vietnam ten years ago.

He remembered me too and was surprised to
see me again after so many years. He con-
gratulated me for getting into OTS and wished
me luck. He really was a good supervisor and
with him making it to the top rank of Chief
Master Sergeant, that was proof that good
things happen to good people.

The last week of May 1972 I got two packages of food from home and a couple of
letters. I called these "care packages" and
they usually had stuff that I couldn't get in
Vietnam. This week I got one of my favorite
Southern foods, Brunswick stew. I also got

some sandwich spread and other things like a pre-sweetened powdered drink mix.

One of the letters had some bad news in it. Daddy's uncle, Dallas Boswell died. He was the brother of my Grandma Crews and my great uncle, Clifford Boswell.

The heavy thunderstorms we got each afternoon the end of May were causing us to stop working. We had to get as much work done in the morning as possible. Four days in a row it had gotten up to 97° so we got wet either from our own sweat or the rain or both. Mildew formed on all of my uniforms and boots I'd left in the barracks. That building wasn't air conditioned so there was no way to control the high humidity.

We got a bit of good news the last week of May. We'd been working 9 days in a row before getting a day off. Starting June 1st, we'd be switching to a 7-on and 1-off schedule. We'd still work a 12-hour shift but there were no complaints from us.

It was about this time that I started doing the paperwork to get married. I don't remember if I proposed to Lin in the traditional way or not, presenting her with an engagement ring. My memory about that is a total blank, no matter how hard I try to remember.

The paperwork to get married was a nightmare. Both countries had their own requirements to be met. There were background investigations, briefings about lots of marriage-related topics to attend, dozens of signatures to get on the forms, fees to pay, etc. I had to go to various Vietnamese government offices to get some things done and various American military and civilian offices to get other things done, including several visits to the American embassy in Saigon. Whenever I see programs on TV showing the American embassy under attack during the 1968 Tet Offensive or the last Americans leaving from the roof via helicopter in 1975 I think back to my visits inside of that building in 1972.

In addition to all the paperwork, I had to talk to my first sergeant, unit commander and a chaplain. I also spoke with GIs who had already gotten married here. I also talked to a GI whose family disowned him for marrying a "Gook" and didn't approve of him marrying a woman from Vietnam. He did so anyway.

The vice-consulate of the U.S. embassy told me about another problem I was facing. If I got transferred to the Philippines before the paperwork was completed here, there would be even more paperwork to do. That was because MACV regulations in Vietnam differed from the requirements of the Philippine government and PACAF (Pacific Air Forces), the U.S. command in charge of the U.S. military forces stationed at Clark Air Base. Some of the PACAF requirements here were the same, but not all.

One plan I came up with in case that happened was to go to Clark Air Base and do whatever paperwork was necessary to complete the requirements to get married. Lin would stay in her apartment in Cholon. I would rent an apartment off base near Clark Air Base and then when Lin was ready to travel with a passport and visa, we'd have a place to live. I'd talked to some guys who were here TDY from Clark and they said apartments near the base were cheap and easy to find.

I had problems with warts growing on my left hand at the end of May. I used a liquid wart remover on them but they just kept growing back. Some of them were big and were being scraped bad enough to bleed whenever I put my leather work gloves on. I

went to the dispensary and had the warts removed. Most were frozen but one had deep
roots and had to be cut out of the back of my
hand. I had several bandaids on my hand and
wouldn't be able to put a glove on so they
gave me a work deferrment authorization to
give to my supervisor. It got me out of
breaking down cargo pallets for a week, and it
kept me from having to lift anything heavy as
well, so my hand could heal properly.

I was given a new job because of that. I
was shown how to work in the pallet yard. I
drove a 10K forklift using only my right hand.
I put the good reusable empty cargo pallets in
stacks in one part of the pallet yard and the
ones in need of repair were put in different
stacks in another part of the pallet yard. A
Vietnamese civilian worked with me, doing the
manual labor. He used a 15-inch long steel
rod to get the pallets lined up. After reaching a certain height, tie-down chains were put
through the metal rings on the corners of the
pallets and they'd be chained together. Then
cargo nets were put over them to keep them
stable. He also put heavy wooden three-point
dunnage between the pallets after several were
stacked on top of eachother so they wouldn't
become warped under too much weight.

I'd then do the paperwork so the pallets
could be flown out on military aircraft. That
included weighing the stacks and putting the
weight on a placard attached to the nets.
After a few weeks of doing that, I became a
real good one-handed forklift driver.

An unusual coincidence happened to me during the last week of May. On my lunch break
one day, I went across the street from the
base to the MACV Headquarters compound. It
was surrounded by barbed wire fences and some
fences that were chain-link and topped with
barbed wire. There were sandbagged gun em-
placements with only a few entrance points.

Someone told me there was a nice snack bar
and a barber shop there and I needed a hair
cut. As I was walking down the hall in that
very large air conditioned building, an Army
Sergeant Major walked up to me. I saw the
name Peterson on his uniform name tag. I'd
attended Wurzburg American High School in
West Germany from December 1966 to my gradu-
ation in June 1969. I knew a guy and his
sister there with the same last name. He
and I were both on the wrestling and soccer
teams and I was one grade ahead of him and
one grade behind his sister.

Sergeant Major Peterson said something
like, "Didn't you graduate from Wurzburg
American High School and then go to college?"
I told him that I did and explained how I
got where I was now. He told me that he was
assigned to the medical clinic at MACV Headquarters and was due to go home in August.
His daughter graduated from college recently
and his son Mark was just finishing his
freshman year in college. We both couldn't
believe what a coincidence this was, seeing
eachother in Germany just a couple of years
ago and now seeing eachother in Vietnam. It
was pure chance and proved once again what a
small world it is that we live in.

While at Tan Son Nhut, I also ran into a
few guys who I'd seen at Sheppard Air Force
Base in Wichita Falls, Texas when I was in
tech school. They had been there in a class
that graduated a week ahead of mine.

I also met a Sergeant at Tan Son Nhut who
had been stationed at Tinker Air Force Base
in Oklahoma City before coming here. We had
a lot to talk about as my youngest brother
was born on that base and I'd gone to school
near there in Midwest City.

Last, but not least, I met a guy at Bien
Hoa who was TDY there for five days. He used
to go to Monmouth, New Jersey to the horse
races and lived near where my Grandma Smith

did, in Toms River, New Jersey. I was born in the Army hospital at Fort Monmouth. Small world indeed!

The fighting was still going on in Quang Tri and An Loc, making the news every day. That's why we had so much work to do here, to make sure the troops in those places got the supplies and equipment they needed. That included every type and calibre of ammunition for their individual weapons and mortars, artillery, helicopters, etc. They were getting some of their supplies from other bases where that stuff had been airlifted too, not just here. It took a lot of people to keep the soldiers on the battlefields supplied.

As May came to an end, many questions that were going through my mind remained unanswered. Would this TDY to Tan Son Nhut be changed to a PCS so I could finish out my tour here? Would I still be going to Clark Air Base, and if so, when? Would all of this paperwork I had to do to get married in Vietnam get finished before I had to leave? Would my family approve of my marriage or would I have to stay in Asia to avoid prejudices I might run into from them or other Americans? What would happen here in South Vietnam after the last American troops left? There was a lot on my mind, a lot of things for a young man of twenty to deal with.
    Then I remembered the words on a poster I'd seen on a neighbor's wall in the barracks back at Bien Hoa, "Today is the first day of the rest of your life." I thought about that and how it might apply to me. I just figured that I'd concentrate on today, what IS, and not worry about things I couldn't control, the WHAT IFs of tomorrow. I'd live life to the fullest, one day at a time, for tomorrow may never come. That's what I got from that poster.

CHAPTER NINE

The month of June started off in an unexpected way. I went back to Bien Hoa with a
friend of mine on my day off. I wanted to
check and see if my assignment to Clark Air
Base was still on hold or not. The Personnel Office folks told me the paperwork was
not there any more and that it may have been
sent to Tan Son Nhut's CBPO.

We went to my old barracks next and found
John Karasek there. He and Armand Fecteau
were my roommates before I left on this TDY.
John told me that the workload was so light
now in his section that he was on a 1 and 1
schedule. He worked one night and had the
next night off. I told him what I'd been
doing at Tan Son Nhut and how lucky he was.

The next day I went to CBPO at Tan Son
Nhut and told them what the people at Bien
Hoa's CBPO had told me about my assignment
paperwork. They checked on it and found
that my assignment was in but the travel orders might not be in for another two to four
weeks. All they could do for me now was let
me know that I'd be assigned to the 604th
MASS (Military Airlift Support Squadron),
Clark Air Base, Philippines. There was no
departure or reporting date yet. It could
be as early as July or as late as October.

A GI friend of mine, his Vietnamese girlfriend and Lin and I went out together to
downtown Saigon one night in early June to
eat in a fancy French restaurant. It was
located inside of a large hotel, one that
had been built by the French in the early
1950s. The restaurant looked very fancy and
expensive to me, like something out of a
movie made twenty years ago because of the
decor that I guessed was the original decor
when the place first opened for business.

The waiters wore white jackets with black
bowties and were the pros at etiquette. I had
lobster with butter sauce, three big ones, and
hot rolls with real butter. We had a small
drink before the meal and I felt like royalty.
The bill for Lin and I only amounted to the
equivalent of $6.00 in Piasters. I couldn't
believe how cheap it was to eat out in Saigon
in good restaurants and there were several
real good ones to choose from. I chose to eat
lobster that night because I'd never eaten any
before and probably never would again in such
a fancy place like that. I couldn't afford to
eat lobster in the U.S. on my low pay.

On June 15, 1972 eighty one civilians were
killed when a bomb exploded inside of their
Cathay Pacific Airways jetliner while it flew
over South Vietnam. The plane carried passengers from Japan, Hong Kong, Thailand, Singapore, Malaysia, Philippines, Bangladesh, Austrailia, England, Ireland, France, Taiwan and
the United States. The plane had left Bangkok
on its way to Hong Kong and investigators said
a woman who got on in Bangkok had the bomb in
her carry-on bag.
The four-engine Convair 880 exploded at
29,000 feet and fell to the ground in three
main pieces about 200 miles northeast of
Saigon. It was shocking news to us in Vietnam. The war was causing the deaths of too
many people in this country already, and now
this. At first I thought maybe a North Vietnamese SAM missile brought the plane down.
Regardless of how it happened, I felt real bad
for all those people.

Around this time in June, I got a three-day
pass. I told my supervisor that I had not
gone on an R & R and I could really use some
time off, especially since my hand was still
healing from having those warts removed and
was still sore. My left hand was healing up,

but very slowly. This break gave me a chance to catch up on letter writing. I wrote a dozen letters between June 18th and 19th, mostly to friends and relatives who had written to me. I felt obligated to answer each letter I received.

On June 23, 1972 I experienced a downpour of rain so hard and fast, it was like standing under a waterfall. It rained for several hours and we had to stop working outside. Visibility was down to a couple of feet and the water in front of our freight office was at least 5 inches deep. It only took 30 minutes of hard rain to reach that level. We actually had some of our heavy pieces of wood used as 3-point dunnage floating across the pavement. I heard that a typhoon was off the coast of Vietnam, giving us heavier-than-normal rains.

Another terrible incident happened in Vietnam in June and it also made headlines around the world. Photos of the tragic incident made it into newspapers and even published in books after the war was over, graphically showing the results of the incident.

Somewhere southwest of Saigon, a South Vietnamese fighter pilot saw a bunch of people running down a road. The nearby town was under attack by North Vietnamese forces and the pilot thought those people were enemy soldiers. He dropped some napalm bombs on them and the burning jellied gasoline killed many of them and injured many of the survivors. The tragic part of this accident was that many innocent civilians, mostly old people and children, were the victims. They had been running away from the battle in their town. They thought the road they were running down led to safety. For many, it led to their deaths. The napalm burned their skin and clothing. The photo in the paper that got the most attention was of a young

naked girl running down a road, along with
other civilians. She had removed her burning
clothing and some people that were near her
had smoke coming from their singed clothing.

Another picture taken of her after she
stopped running, showed her back all burned
and others in the photo were screaming and
crying as she was. It was another "friendly
fire" incident.

Many years later, I saw another picture of
the same girl and her story in a newspaper.
She was an adult in the photo. The day she
got burned, she'd been put on a medi-vac
helicopter and flown to a field hospital and
then on to the United States for treatment.
Some doctors did skin graft surgery on her
and she was looking normal again in the
latest photo. She never returned to Vietnam
and she was one of the luckier ones.

By June 18, 1972 my left hand was almost
completely healed. There were only some pink
spots where the warts had been. Even though
I was physically capable of removing cargo
nets from pallets and lifting boxes by hand
as I'd been doing before having the warts removed, I continued driving a forklift in the
pallet yard. I let my supervisor know that I
didn't want to work in air freight and wanted
to return to my Passenger Service career
field I'd originally been in. He told me
that as long as I was TDY here, I'd continue
doing the same job.

Also, when some of the guys that were permanently assigned here left in August, I was
going to be put in charge of the pallet yard.
He said I'd done such a good job, including
doing all of the associated paperwork that
goes with shipping stacks of good and bad
cargo pallets, that he felt confident that I
could be in charge of it and make sure things
continued to be done right. He really knew
how to turn a negative into a positive and I

admit it helped with my attitude then and
even later in my career.

On my way to and from work each day, I
passed by a large Pan American World Airways
(Pan Am) billboard across the street from
the U.S. Army's 3rd Field Hospital. It had
rained so much during the first three weeks
of June that the empty field next to that
big sign was flooded. I saw some kids swimming near the billboard a few days during
breaks in the rain and when the tallest kid
stood up, the water was waist-deep on him.
That was a big field and it took a lot of
rain to fill it up deep enough for them to
swim in.

A couple of my friends went back to the
States on short notice near the end of June.
One of them was contacted by the American
Red Cross that his grandmother was very ill.
He went home for two weeks. My other friend
I'd known since tech school, got even worse
news. They notified him that his grand-
mother had died three days ago and he left
too. At least he didn't have to wait long
for a flight out of here.

There was no such thing as mandatory
"Surepay" back then, when your paycheck
went straight to the bank. I had to go to
the orderly room each payday and sign a form
to get my paycheck. Then I'd go to Accounting and Finance to cash it and sometimes buy
a money order to send some of it home. They
paid us with MPC (Military Payment Certificates) which we called funny money or Monop-
oly money because it looked nothing like
green American dollars. For years, MPC even
replaced coins so coins were made out of
paper. In 1972 MPC only replaced dollar
bills. We were allowed to use American coins
because there were snack and soda machines on

a lot of bases.

Imagine my surprise when I went to pick up my paycheck the end of June and there wasn't one there for me. Nor were there any for any of the rest of the guys TDY from Bien Hoa. To add insult to injury, we weren't allowed to return to Bien Hoa to see if our paychecks were there either. I don't remember who came up with the idea to get our former commander at Bien Hoa to help us but I'm sure glad somebody thought of it.

Lieutenant Colonel Crutchfield was back in Vietnam doing another tour and he was the Station Traffic Manager here at Tan Son Nhut. We all went to see him and explained our problem and lack of help by people here to get our pay. Coincidentally, he didn't get his check either so that put him in a position to be sympathetic towards us and our situation.

He called the OIC of Finance at Bien Hoa and told him to get somebody over here with our paychecks ASAP! He told us that he would personally drive three of us at a time to Bien Hoa so we could fill out travel vouchers and get paid for being TDY if the checks didn't arrive soon. With the prodding of his phone call, we all got paid and he didn't have to do any driving. We all thanked him and beyond that, we admired him for his willingness to help us out when others just said, "We can't do anything because you're TDY and don't belong to our organization" or some other excuse.

The event in June 1972 that had the biggest affect on me was when Lin told me that she was pregnant and I was going to become a father. The paperwork to get married was already begun so this news added a twist to things. It's been so many years since then, I can't recall how I felt about it.

I know I wrote a long letter home about it. I was motivated to do my best to prepare Lin for life in America and prepare my parents for

a daughter-in-law and a grandchild.   That was
a tall order for me, a very big challenge.   I
asked for their help with several things and
they came through for me.   They sent me a
blender, a cookbook with lots of photos and
some magazines showing life in America.   I
wanted Lin to learn how to cook some American
food and to see how Americans lived and what
our country looked like.

CHAPTER TEN

July started out with an unusual situation
that happened near where I worked. On July
2nd I went to lunch and up until then everything was normal. Right after returning to
work, I had to drive a forklift down the side
of the runway to the carpenter shop. That's
where we got our dunnage, those thick pieces
of wood used for separating pallets when
they were being stacked for shipment to other
places.

As I began my turn from where the pallet
yard was, to get along side the runway heading towards the carpenter shop, I saw a huge
Pan Am 747. It was parked on the ramp where
planes like that normally parked. But something wasn't normal. This particular plane
had all of its escape slides hanging to the
ground. Passengers, some with hand-held
luggage, were sliding to the ground, which
was quite a distance from the doors of the
747.

There were MPs (military police) with M-16s
all around and I just had to pull over and
stop driving long enough to find out what was
going on. I found out that a Vietnamese man
had tried to hijack the plane to Hanoi, the
capital of North Vietnam.

The pilot told the hijacker that he had to
land for fuel and get permission to cross the
DMZ so they wouldn't be shot down by North
Vietnamese planes. The DMZ was the border
between the two countries, called the demilitarized zone.

When the plane landed at Tan Son Nhut Air
Base, which also served as the international
airport for Saigon, the hijacker held a 10-
inch knife to the throat of a stewardess and
said that he had a bomb. Later on it was
discovered that the bomb was only two lemons
wrapped up in aluminum foil. Boy, talk about

a plan that went sour!

The pilot of the 747 weighed about 200 pounds and the hijacker, around 135. He was a lot shorter than the pilot too. The pilot thought that he could take advantage of his larger size. When he went into the cabin to talk to the hijacker, he overpowered him with a headlock and proceeded to choke him.

A policeman in civilian clothes then shot the hijacker five times while the pilot held him and then the pilot threw the hijacker out of an open door. The hijacker hit the pavement like a sack of potatoes. If the bullets hadn't killed him, the long fall to the pavement certainly would have. That was a long drop!

A few passengers got hurt when they slid down the long escape slides. One Lieutenant Colonel in the U.S. Air Force suffered a broken leg. The flight crew had left the engines running while the passengers got out. Some of the passengers that slid down behind the engines were blown off the slides and fell onto the pavement of the parking ramp. Those 747s have huge, powerful engines. You could stand up inside the front end of one and stretch with your hands over your head and you still wouldn't be able to touch the top of the engine.

That was one front-page news story that I witnessed in Vietnam. The pilot of the 747 and the cop who shot the hijacker were heros in my mind. That proved to me, once again, you just never know what might happen in a war zone.

Some friends of mine who worked in the Line Loading section of Air Freight told me about seeing some dismembered bodies in body bags, the black plastic ones that zipped closed. I'm glad I didn't, but I did see three metal caskets on pallets (one on each separate pallet) that had signs on them. The

signs said, "Do not leave in sun. Bodies
have not been embalmed." Even through the
metal and plastic body bags, I could smell
the sickening smell of death from a few feet
away. I was glad that I didn't have to work
in a job where I'd have to transport bodies
from the field. I didn't think I could
stomach it.

One day as I was walking from the latrine
back to my work area, I saw an Air Force
Master Sergeant (E-7) on a smoke break. He
was standing near a cargo pallet that had a
dead body on it, inside of a black plastic
body bag. He was standing with one foot on
the pallet and the other on the pavement and
he was facing away from the body. He probably didn't realize it but he was being dis-
respectful to the deceased Korean soldier.

I was getting closer to the Master Sergeant and I knew something was wrong when a
Korean soldier walked towards him from off to
my right where some offices were located.
The Korean soldier had an M-16 rifle and I
saw and heard him chamber a round as he walked towards the sergeant. The soldier had an
angry scowl on his face. As soon as the
sound of the round of ammo being chambered
got the attention of the senior NCO, the
American took his foot off of the pallet and
began walking away from the Korean. I think
he realized then that he'd messed up.

I thought that maybe the Korean soldier,
called ROKs, pronounced like rocks by American GIs, was a friend of the one in the body
bag and was there to escort him back to
South Korea for burial. ROK stood for Republic of Korea, and the VC feared them because
of their tenaciousness on the battlefield.
He took offense to the American NCO who put
his foot up on the pallet near where his dead
friend was and was about to let the American
know just how offended he was. I walked to
the left of the pallet on my way back to my

work area and made a mental note to never put
my foot on a pallet containing a body bag, no
matter what country they were from.

By the first week of July 1972, the Communist Easter Offensive was turning into a defensive struggle for the enemy for the most
part. An Loc had been retaken by the South
Vietnamese and American forces and our forces
were only about three miles away from Quang
Tri City. Many captured enemy weapons were
displayed each night on the TV news, especially tanks and armored personnel carriers.
     July 3, 1972 was a Monday. Because of the
rain showers we were getting, the high was
only 86° and the low was 80°. The humidity
was terribly high even with lower day time
temperatures. By the end of each day, my
uniform was soaked in sweat and rainwater.
Staying dry while working outdoors was impossible.
     When I got off work, one of my favorite
things to do was watch people from the balcony just outside my apartment. From there
I had a good view of the narrow street that
my apartment was on. It ran through a
neighborhood that consisted of multi-story
apartment buildings. Most of them were
three or four stories tall.
     Vendors with wheeled carts with handles
that made it possible to move them around
from place to place by one person were on
this narrow street every day. That's how I
came to learn about something I'd never experienced in America before, street food.
It was literally food that was prepared,
sold, and often eaten in the street. Some
of it was exotic like dried squid cooked over
coals or pots of rice and pots of soup made
from vegetables and fish parts. Other vendors sold great-smelling breads and rolls,
kept warm in wicker baskets.
     My favorite street food was a Chinese-

style vegetable and meatball soup. The meat-
balls were small, like an average-size marble.
When I told my friends about it, they teased
me and said those were monkey balls and they
called it monkey ball soup. It was a known
fact that monkey meat was consumed in this
country but whatever it was, cat, rat, bat or
monkey, it was good and I ate it. When in
Rome, do as the Romans do, I'd been told. So
pass the monkey ball soup over here, please.
Mmmm, good!

I think I must have tried just about everything sold off of vendor's carts while living
in that apartment in Saigon. I remember eating dried squid on a stick with BBQ sauce
brushed on it with a small paint brush. It
was like eating beef jerky, very tough and
chewy, but still good. I didn't like the
Vietnamese version of BBQ sauce though. It
was more like banana ketchup, something used
as a condiment here and in the Philippines.

Sometimes on my day off if the weather was
bad or if Lin didn't want to go out, I'd watch
her and several of her female friends who
lived in the apartment building play a game
I'd never seen played before. It was Mahjong,
played with 144 little ivory-colored game
pieces about the size of dominoes. They had
Chinese characters printed on them in black
ink. They would play for many hours and I'd
listen to them talking and watch their moves
but I never learned how to play the game.

The first week of July 1972 ended badly
for us. First, Lin had a brother killed near
Quang Tri. He was in the South Vietnamese
Army and his unit was in the big battle going
on there. Then her mother had to be operated
on and almost died. Lin spent the night at
the hospital the day her mother went there.
When she returned to our apartment, she told
me that her mother would recover and be OK.

On the morning of July 8th as I was walk-

ing to work, I got run over by a motorcycle.
I was on a sidewalk, walking towards Tan Son
Nhut Air Base, already having passed by the
big U.S. Army 3rd Field Hospital. The highway I had to cross to get to the gate near
MACV Headquarters and on to my workcenter
was a divided one with a raised curb in the
middle. On the side I was on, the traffic
was all going away from the base and on the
other side of the divider, the traffic was
all going towards the base and other parts
of the city of Saigon.

Before leaving the sidewalk to cross the
road, I looked to my left where the traffic
was stopped at a red light down the street.
There was no need for me to look to my right
until I reached the divider in between the
lanes of traffic. In Saigon, people on
motorcycles, pedi-cabs, cars, trucks and
buses squeezed into any available space they
could find on the roads. They didn't always
drive with one vehicle behind the other in
traffic lanes like we did in America. There
was a solid wall of vehicles at that red
light, lined up from curb to curb like a
giant tidal wave of vehicles, waiting for the
light to turn green.

I saw my chance to cross the street. No
sooner had I taken my first step into the
street then BAM! Something hit me hard on
my right side and I spun around once and then
fell into the street. I looked up and saw a
Vietnamese military policeman, the ones we
Americans called "white mice" because of
their small size and their white helmets with
the black letters "QC" on them, riding away
from me on a small motorcycle. He was traveling the wrong way, against the traffic,
right up next to the curb. He just kept going after running me over.

I got up as quickly as I could because the
light down the street had turned green and
that solid wall of vehicles was heading right

towards me. I literally ran for my life to
reach the relative safety of the divider. I
would have been run over by dozens of vehicles had I not made it, of that I'm sure. My
upper right thigh and right hip were hurting.
I limped the rest of the way to work and then
went to the dispensary to get checked out.
All things considered, I was lucky to be
alive.

My pants were dirty and I had a scratch
and bruise on my right leg. A little blood
was draining in my leg muscles and the doctor
told me to put a hot towel on that spot four
times a day. Two X-rays were taken and I had
no broken bones but I was very sore.

I was given a medical duty excuse for the
day and after showing that to my supervisor
and telling him what the doctor told me to do
I went back to my apartment. Twenty years to
the day earlier, on July 8, 1952, my biological father died in the Korean War. What a
bizarre coincidence, for me to have had a
near-death experience exactly twenty years to
the day after his death.

The next day the electricity in our apartment building went off and stayed off for a
long time. There was an electrical fire in a
building down the street and we used the
power outage as an excuse to have a candle-
light dinner. Every war has its' romantic
moments.

That same day, Lin was injured in an accident. She was riding on the back of a motorcycle to visit her mother and a car hit the
motorcycle. The big toe of her right foot
was forced into the spokes of the wheel on
the motorcycle and it was a gory mess to look
at. There was nothing left of her toenail
but at least no bones were broken. I had to
convince her to go to a doctor and get medical treatment. She was planning on treating
the injury herself.

Most Vietnamese couldn't afford a car so there were small 50cc motorcycles everywhere. I'd even seen a family of four riding on one. What caused her accident was the fact that passing on the right was legal here. So, if you were going to make a right turn, you had to check and make sure nobody was trying to pass you on the right. Her driver failed to do that.

You could take a taxi anywhere in Saigon for only 200 Piasters, about 50¢, but Lin was thrifty and took a motorcycle ride instead because it was cheaper than a taxi. I told her that from now on she would take a taxi. Her foot was all bandaged up for awhile so she didn't have a choice now.

Even with her foot bandaged, Lin still managed to do everything she always did before the accident happened. She still swept the floor and kept our apartment clean and did the laundy by hand, in the shower part of the bathroom. There were no coin laundrys or washers or dryers in this building or nearby. She also went shopping in the market but only by taxi now.

Later that week I had to take her on base to get her passport photo taken. She also had to get a pre-marital physical exam, X-rays, blood tests, and more marriage paperwork to do.

My workload increased in the pallet yard around this time. We used to have to chain all of the bad pallets together on top of a good one so they could be flown to Travis Air Force Base in California for repairs or for destruction. Somebody decided that the procedures needed to be changed and the bad pallets were going to be sent by ship now instead of by plane.

That caused me and the Vietnamese man known as Papa-san to remove 160 chains and 40 straps from the 20 stacks of pallets that we had worked so hard to prepare for air ship-

ment. Then we had to put metal bands with
metal clamps on them after they were broken
down into stacks of ten pallets.

Sometime during July 1972, the actress
turned anti-war activist Jane Fonda, daughter of film star Henry Fonda, went to North
Vietnam. She was photographed and filmed in
the North while wearing a North Vietnamese
Army helmet while sitting on an anti-aircraft
gun. While at that fully-manned gun, she
sang an anti-war song for the cameras and
crowd.
While she was doing that, some American
POWs (Prisoners Of War) were being tortured
by their North Vietnamese prison guards. The
POWs had refused to pose with her in front of
the cameras or to meet with her. That was
another event that made headline news while I
was in Vietnam.

There were now fewer than 5,000 U.S. advisors on duty with ARVN (Army of the Republic of Vietnam) units. There were only two
large U.S. Army units still in Vietnam at
this time. The 1st Battalion of the 7th
Cavalry Division and the 3rd Battalion of
the 21st Infantry Division were the last
large fighting units still here. There were
many smaller units still scattered around the
country like my own but it was apparent that
it would soon be an all-Vietnamese war.

In addition to vendors selling street food
in Saigon, I saw other things being sold on
the streets as well. One day while walking
home from work, a young man asked me if I
wanted to buy some drugs. After telling him
no, he then asked me if I wanted to buy a
knife. He opened his outer shirt and showed
me a bunch of different types and sizes of
knives that were attached to the inside of
his shirt. He pulled out a knife, pushed on

a small button, and out popped a long blade.
It was a switchblade knife. He held it out
to me to inspect and offered it to me at a
low price. I decided to buy it for my own
personal protection. A few times I'd been
approached by some men that looked like they
were up to no good as I walked down the
sidewalk going to and from work. One incident happened to me not too long ago that
also caused me to decide to buy the knife
for protection.

One day I was riding in the front of a 3-
wheeled taxi with a case of soda in my lap.
The driver sat behind me on the part of this
vehicle that was the back half of a motorcycle. The front part where passengers sat
could hold two people sitting side-by-side.
The two front tires were on either side of
the passengers. There was nothing but air
in front of the passengers and there, sadly,
were no seatbelts.

The watch I wore at the time had a
stretchable metal wristband and was on my
left arm. As we drove down the street, a
motorcycle with two men on it pulled along
side of me. The guy on the back reached
over and grabbed my watchband and tried to
pull it off. All I could do with my hands
full was lean away from him and yell, "Dee
dee mau," which means either go quickly or
get out of here, depending on the situation
and voice inflection. He couldn't get my
watch and gave up after a few seconds.

They drove ahead of us and then the guy
on the back was shot off the motorcycle by a
policeman on the sidewalk nearby who saw
what was going on. The driver of the motorcycle managed to drive away as his passenger
tumbled to the side of the road. I thought
to myself, now that's justice!

Guys that rode around on their motorcycles
in pairs and stole from people were known as
"cowboys." That was another reason I bought

the knife. I was glad the police were there
that day but knew they couldn't be everywhere
all the time.

Another terrible thing happened that July
near my apartment in Saigon. I came home
from work one day and Lin, along with several
other women, were standing around out in the
street crying. I asked her what was wrong and
she told me what happened right across the
street from our building.
She and these other women were all friends
of two sisters who lived together in an apartment on the other side of our narrow street.
One of the sisters had a boyfriend who was an
American civilian working in Saigon. She was
blind and very pretty, according to Lin. I'd
never seen her in person, or her boyfriend or
sister either. Sometimes one of her friends
would take the blind sister to the market and
help her with her grocery shopping.
The pretty young blind sister came home
from shopping that day and discovered her boyfriend in bed with her sister. After an argu-
ment with both of them, the blind sister jumped from the top floor of the building into the
narrow street below and killed herself. She
felt betrayed and besides breaking her heart,
the betrayal broke her spirit and will to live.
It was another sad day in Saigon.

I celebrated my 21st birthday with Lin on
July 14, 1972. My birthday cake consisted of a
box full of little square individually-wrapped
brownies that my parents sent me. After un-
wrapping the plastic from each one, the brownies were arranged on a plate to resemble a
cake. I also received some candles and some
candy letters to put on it that spelled out
"HAPPY BIRTHDAY." Mom and Dad's thoughtfulness
really made it a very special day for me.
Until now, I couldn't vote for my own commander-in-chief who was at the top of my chain

of command. My destiny was in his hands.
Now that I was 21 years old and could vote,
his destiny would be in my hands. Until now
I couldn't go to a bar in my own country and
buy a drink even though I had sworn to defend it and die for it if necessary in this
undeclared war. With the change of a single
day on the calendar, all that had changed.

One day around the middle of July when
things were a little slow and I was on a
break at work, I walked over to a group of
six coffins that had just come in from the
field. I read the names on the paperwork
that was attached to each coffin. One of
them had the rank of O-7 next to the name
and I didn't know what that stood for.
There was a story the very next day in
the Pacific Stars and Stripes newspaper
about an American one-star general (Brigi-
dier General is a one-star) who was killed
at the battle for An Loc. An artillery
shell exploded about fifteen feet away from
him. They had a picture of him with the
story and I recognized his name as the one
I'd seen on the coffin with the O-7 rank on
it just one day prior. That's how I found
out what O-7 stood for.
You might ask, who goes around looking at
names on caskets? Well, I had an uncle, a
cousin and the father of one of my high
school friends who either had been or were
still in Vietnam, and there might be others
I knew there as well so I wanted to find out
if it was anyone I knew in one of those caskets. I suppose my curiosity level was
higher than that of other people.
After seeing legless and armless men who
were former South Vietnamese soldiers begg-
ing for money every day just outside the
base gate I went through every day, I guess
I might have become a little bit desensitiz-
ed towards things that other people would be

affected by, like looking at the names on coffins. War does different things to different people. I thought that what I did was perfectly normal and it didn't bother me one bit.

In previous wars our country has been in, including the Civil War, names of soldiers who had been killed in battle used to be posted on a list in public places for all to see. We didn't have any lists of names to look at where I worked in Vietnam so I did the next best thing in my mind to find out if one of my friends or relatives was in one of those six caskets. That's the only way I know how to explain my actions then.

Lin and I got the results of the X-rays and blood tests and even her passport pictures back only a few days after having been on base to do all those things. So far, everything had gone well and the biggest thing we were waiting for so we could get married was the background investigation done by both governments.

The Vietnamese national police raided our apartment building one evening. They told the tenants that they were looking for deserters from the American and South Vietnamese armed forces and demanded that everyone leave their apartments and show their IDs to them out there in the street. Lin whispered to me that they were dishonest cops and were conducting a shake-down, trying to get the tenants to pay them money so they would leave them alone. The national police would arrest people for the slightest little thing and get money from them so they'd be set free again if they were arrested.

We were up on the third floor so Lin had some advance warning about what was going on. The entrance to our apartment was at the end of the outside walkway, almost like a long

narrow balcony, unlike the other apartment
entrances which were on the inside stairwell
of the building. She told me to turn off the
lights, hide in the bathroom and don't make a
sound. We both hid there and we could hear
the police talking loudly to the tenants
while they made their demands. They didn't
sound very friendly. I couldn't understand
what they were saying but Lin told me in a
low whisper. To say that I was scared and
nervous would be an understatement.

I'd heard some stories about how people
got beat up by the Vietnamese national police
and how terrible the conditions were in their
jails. It didn't matter if you were an American or not, except for one thing. The money
they wanted from Americans was much more than
what they demanded from Vietnamese because
they knew we got paid a lot more than they
did. With only two stripes on my uniform, I
made as much per month as a Vietnamese Army
Lieutenant Colonel.

The police never found the entrance to our
apartment and none of our neighbors told them
about us either. We were so relieved when
they left. Lin talked to some of our neighbors and sure enough, some of them had to pay
the crooked police a bribe to keep from being
arrested on some trumped-up charges. They
found no deserters.

I don't remember exactly when we moved out
of our apartment. It was sometime during the
third week of July. We rented it on a month-
by-month basis and when it came time to pay
for another month, we decided not to. We
knew by now that I'd be returning to Bien Hoa
soon. The decision had been made to send me
and the other guys who were TDY back there
again at the end of this month. My supervisor told me that a TDY could only last for
89 days without being changed to a PCS and
someone in our chain of command had decided
to not permanently assign us to Tan Son Nhut.

We took most of our things to Lin's two-
room house in Cholon. Then we rented a room
in the Federal Hotel for a couple of days.
We had a room with a small balcony on the
second floor. The hotel was on a narrow side
street with apartment buildings full of Vietnamese families across the street. There was
a market nearby and Lin would go there by
herself to buy our prepared meals and soft
drinks. Street food vendors were abundant in
the market and we got good food at a low
price, especially my favorite, monkey ball
soup.

The national police raided the Federal
Hotel one night only a short time after raid-
ing our apartment building on the other side
of the city. They were looking for deserters
too, so they said, but we knew better.
The corrupt police were just trying to get
people to pay them off so they would leave
them alone. The hotel manager came to our
room and other guest's rooms as well to ask
for some money to help pay the police so they
wouldn't come inside the hotel and harass us.
We made a small contribution to the pay-off
fund. The police accepted the money and left
but only after making threats and scaring us
half to death. We had turned the lights off
and hid in the bathroom and waited quietly
until they were gone. Once again, no deserters were found.

I was happy to be returning to Bien Hoa
because I thought I'd get to work in a Passenger Service job once again. However, I was
sad about leaving Tan Son Nhut because I'd
gotten used to being with Lin every day and
I'd miss her a lot. Day off visits wouldn't
be the same but I was sure we'd get to see
eachother again, just not sure how often. I
would also miss the extra TDY pay of $2.00
per day in my paycheck. $2.00 went a long
way in Vietnam in those days when changed

into Piasters.

I had to stay in the barracks my last
couple of days at Tan Son Nhut. On Friday,
our TDY group was told that a bus would come
from Bien Hoa and pick us up at our barracks
on Monday. After that, a sergeant from Bien
Hoa came here and told us to be packed and
ready to leave any time between Friday and
Monday. Because of the uncertainty of our
departure, we were all excused from duty and
told to stay by the barracks and watch for
the bus. That was typical of the military;
hurry up and wait.

Right before I left for Bien Hoa, Lin and
I talked and decided to get married in the
base chapel there. All of my friends would
be there and her family too. We'd done
everything the paperwork from the two governments required us to do. Now we had to wait
until they told us we could actually have the
ceremony and that meant that we couldn't set
a date yet. That was very frustrating.

A friend of mine at Tan Son Nhut showed me
his Vietnamese wife's passport and visa he'd
gotten at the American embassy in Saigon. He
was going to be taking his wife's child (not
his biological child) back to the U.S. too.
So far I'd met five GIs married to Vietnamese
women and they all seemed to be happy with
their decisions. They gave me moral support
and their encouraging words gave me hope that
everything would turn out well.

On July 31, 1972 at 0900, my TDY to Tan
Son Nhut Air Base ended. The small blue Air
Force bus from Bien Hoa Air Base picked up
the group of eight I was part of at the barracks. When we arrived back at Bien Hoa, we
were in for a surprise. Passenger Service
operations were then almost non-existant.

There were no more commercial airlines
flights in or out of Bien Hoa any longer. I
was told that some of the airline's planes

had been hit by ground fire and they refused
to fly into Bien Hoa because of that. Therefore, anyone from here that needed to fly back
to the United States for any reason, had to go
to Tan Son Nhut now for a flight.

My new supervisor informed me I'd start
working in the Air Freight Section the next
day. So much for returning to Passenger Service. The guys here were on 12-hour shifts
and I'd be working from 6 a.m.-6 p.m. The
good news was, their workload was lighter than
Tan Son Nhut's had been and they were on a 4
and 2 schedule. That meant they worked four
days in a row and then got two days off. I
liked that part!

Since I wasn't going to be returning to
Passenger Service work like when I worked in
Tri-Service ATCO, gone were the days of playing bad jokes on departing Army "grunts",
like throwing rocks up on the tin roof of the
terminal and watching them dive to the ground,
thinking the loud BANGS on the roof was "incoming." And gone were the nights when my
co-workers would hold me upside-down over the
amnesty box so I could reach through the
narrow door on the top and get Army-issue
silver pocket knives from it, among other
items of interest.

In the middle of the night on night shift,
the passenger terminal was usually empty except for those who worked there and got
bored sometimes, like my friends and I.

People were allowed to drop off things into the amnesty box before going through Customs without fear of getting into trouble for
having things that might get them into
trouble if the items were discovered by the
Army Customs people. They used drug-sniffing
German Sheppards on passenger's hand-carried
baggage too and caught people using tooth-
paste tubes to mask the smell of the drugs
they tried smuggling back to the U.S. with
them. I saw things like that happen when I

worked in Passenger Service before. We saw
all kinds of stuff in the amnesty box.
There were drugs, knives, decks of cards with
nude photos on them, live ammunition, just to
name a few of the things we saw. We just
wanted the pocket knives that were silver in
color and had U.S. Army engraved on them.
There were several of them at the bottom of
the amnesty box and I was the only guy
skinny enough and light enough to be picked
up and turned upside-down to get my narrow
shoulder (only one would fit) and one arm
down inside the opening at the top of the
wooden box.

We weren't allowed to have guns for our
protection in the barracks so we had to use
something else and those pocket knives were
better than nothing. The barracks of other
Aerial Port units in the country had been
attacked and we aimed to fight back any way
we could if our barracks was ever targeted.

CHAPTER ELEVEN

AUGUST 1972

All hell broke loose across Bien Hoa Air
Base and nearby Bien Hoa City at 5:15 a.m. on
August 1, 1972. I'd set my alarm clock to go
off at 5:30   so I could be at work at my new
job by 6. I was still sound asleep when the
day started out with a BANG, literally. I was
knocked out of bed by the concussion from a
six foot tall 122mm Russian-made rocket which
exploded across the street from my barracks.
The noise from the multiple explosions was
very loud and even though some explosions were
occurring randomly all over the base, every
once in a while, I could hear some which
started at a distance, then followed by others
which came progressively nearer. A unit of
the North Vietnamese Army was walking mortars
across the base. I later confirmed this and
took some pictures showing several hits in a
line across the aircraft parking ramp near
where I would be working.
Paperback books and bug spray cans were
knocked off my wall shelves and added to the
noise coming from outside.
I wasn't hurt by the fall to the concrete
floor. It was only a short distance from my
standard-issue GI bunkbed and I had the
bottom bunk. I just instinctively rolled under the bed until I reached the room's outer
wall. I did this so quickly that I forgot to
grab my helmet and flak jacket that were hanging from a nail in the wall only a few feet
away.
I had crawled to the safety of the wall because on the outside of the building there
were huge cement slabs leaning up against the
walls of the barracks. They were about six
inches thick and about four feet high. They
offered excellent protection from all but a
direct hit. I was hoping that the bed would
protect me from anything that might hit from

above.

Everyone had a roommate when I was assigned to this barracks the previous October.
Now the detachment had a lot fewer members
than before, so we were able to have a room
to ourselves. I'm not sure if the Marines on
the second floor had that privilege. When I
left here in May, these Marines were not here
yet. Because the wooden shelters near our
barracks were falling apart and boarded up,
the Marines had to run down the stairs on the
outside of the two-story building and then
take shelter from the attack in the ground
floor hallway.

There were several more near-misses after
I'd crawled under my bed and I really started
to get nervous. This was the first time that
I ever prayed during an attack. "Please God,
make it stop! This is getting too close!"
We'd been attacked before, but not with so
many mortars and rockets as this, and not as
close to me as this either. I knew things
were getting bad because I could hear secondary explosions and lots of yelling going on
throughout the building.

When I heard some of the young Marines in
the hallway right outside my door start crying, I thought to myself, "These guys are
here to protect me and they can't even take
this. What am I going to do now? I thought
Marines were trained for this kind of thing!"
I hoped the enemy wouldn't start a ground
attack. We'd be in serious trouble if they
did.

One thing that really stands out in my
mind about this particular attack was how
long it lasted. Usually, we'd get a few rockets and mortars and after a minute or two it
would be over. This attack was at least fifteen minutes long. There were continuous explosions as round after round hit the base.

Before the last explosions were over, when
it sounded like the Vietnamese side of the

base was getting the worst of it, one of my
old roommates stuck his head in my room and
said that the Airmen's Club had been hit and
to come out and see. I said, "You're crazy.
I'm not going out there and get killed!" And
he told me that this side of the base wasn't
under attack any more. The explosions did
sound much further away at this time, so I
got up and followed him outside. By then,
most of the Marines who had been in the hallway were getting up and a couple of them were
standing just outside the exit at the end of
the hallway.

We looked up the street in the direction
of the Airmen's Club. It was only about two
blocks away, around 75 yards, so it was easy
to see the smoke and flames. There were some
small explosions coming from the fire, so we
didn't venture any closer.

I went back to my room and got my uniform
on because I'd been wearing shorts at first
and thought I might have to work. I got my
camera too. My friend and I waited until we
were certain the attack was over before we
went back outside again. We went straight to
the passenger terminal, which was only a few
blocks away, in the opposite direction from
the Airmen's Club.

The terminal was a mess! The large metal
building used to have hanging ceiling fans
spread evenly from one end to the other. A
few were on the floor now and several of them
were damaged with fan blades missing or bent.
There was a big hole on the back (flightline)
side of the building, right next to the OIC's
(Officer-In-Charge) office. It looked like a
rocket had hit a steel support beam right
above one of the doors and tore a very large
hole in the roof and in the back of the
building. The windows had been blown out of
the OIC's office as well. Almost all of the
metal wall between two support beams was now
missing, with a gaping hole overhead of at

least forty square feet. Beneath this large
hole was a big pool of dark, almost dried,
blood.

Each morning, one of the U.S. Army Customs
Inspectors who worked in the passenger terminal would walk around the building and collect the money that had been placed in the
orphanage collection boxes located on a
couple of the walls. A lot of GIs leaving
Vietnam had some Piasters or Military Payment
Certificates (MPC) that they didn't want or
need and would drop it in one of the boxes.

Unfortunately, the guy making the rounds
that morning happened to be directly under
where the rocket hit and shrapnel hit him in
the neck. He was put on a helicopter and
flown to the 3rd Field Hospital in Saigon. I
was told by one of his friends in Customs
that he died on the way there, having bled to
death from the neck wound. From the amount
of blood I'd seen on the floor of the terminal, he'd lost a lot of blood before anyone
came to his aid.

I asked the Customs guy why they didn't
take him to the dispensary here on base and
he said that it had been hit too. I checked
in with my supervisor to see if it was OK to
go around and take some pictures of the damage around the base. Since all plane flights
in and out of the base had been stopped because of the attack, he said it was OK. So
our next stop was going to be the dispensary,
a few blocks away from the passenger terminal.

However, before starting the walk over
there, we looked out behind the terminal and
I could see several hits to the flightline. I
thought it would make a good picture, proof of
mortars being used in the attack, in addition
to the rockets. I knew they could be fired
and adjusted if the explosions could be seen
by an enemy observer and these small craters
and burn marks in the flightline were indica-
tions that the gunner was "walking" the mortar

rounds across the base.

The Detachment OIC's blue pickup truck was nearby and there was a hole in the cab. It was between the door frame on the driver's side and the back window. It's a good thing nobody had been sitting in it during the attack. It gave me an eerie feeling. My friend and I had both driven around in that truck before and the hole was at head level.

There was also a hole about the size of a quarter in the wall in the Air Freight building nearby and I took a picture of that right after I took a picture of the hole in the pickup truck. We looked around some more to see if there was more damage in this area.

As we turned back towards the direction of the dispensary, my friend called my attention to a couple of planes that were parked on the ramp behind the terminal. One was an RB-77 and it had a flat tire. The other was a C-7 Caribou and the cargo ramp had been blown off and was on the ground behind it. All of its' tires were flat and it was leaking fuel. I took pictures of both planes. I felt like a war correspondent, removed from my real role in the war, just there to take pictures and report on what I saw. I was getting some good pictures and if I'd written a story for a newspaper or magazine, I would have given it the title:" Bad Day at Bien Hoa." It had been attacked before during my tour, but nothing even close to this, and we were just getting started looking for damage. We didn't have to look far because damage was everywhere around us.

It was a typical hot and humid day and we were soaked in sweat after covering only half the distance to the dispensary. At that point we were on the street behind the BX (Base Exchange) and we could clearly see the damage that had been done to the stacks of palletized beer and soda supplies in the fenced storage area. There were loose cans all over the

place, some still spewing out their contents.
This liquid was draining into a cement drainage ditch located between the storage area
and the base chapel. Because of the direct
hit that resulted in big losses in beer and
soda, the BX had to ration its sales to
everyone for awhile.

The white wooden fence behind the chapel
was splintered quite a bit by the nearby explosions. Some of the fence lay in the
drainage ditch, having been knocked away
from the chapel and showing damage from two
directions.

Four of the rear windows of the chapel
were knocked out and the curtains were burned by the hot shrapnel that penetrated them.
I took a picture of the damaged rear of the
chapel and then went around to the front. I
saw several holes there and a wall panel
that was blown loose. Our place of worship
had been shot through both sides. It was
literally a miracle that nobody was in there
because there were holes in it from front to
back. If a service had been taking place
during the attack, there would have been many
casualties.

We finally reached the dispensary and
most of the damage seemed to be on one side.
An entire wall was lying on the ground, with
a window air conditioner right in the middle
of the hole in the ground created by a rocket
or mortar that hit just a couple of feet away
from the edge of the building. The room that
suffered the most damage was the clinic break-
room. With one of its walls blown out, you
could see everything inside. It was a real
mess inside too. Fortunately, nobody in the
dispensary was injured.

After leaving that location with another
picture having been taken, we decided to walk
over to the flightline and see what else had
been hit in the attack. We were walking away
from the passenger terminal side of the base,

which was at one end of the runway, and headed
towards the covered revetments where the
fighter planes were parked. They were still a
long way off, in the opposite direction.

There were many rows of covered revetments
at Bien Hoa Air Base. Each one housed a plane
of one type or another. We walked past several rows of them before we came to one that
had been damaged. The rounded top had large
cracks in the cement slabs that covered the
steel inner part. There was a very small hole
in the inner steel, where a piece of the rocket or mortar had somehow penetrated. In the
center of the concrete floor where a plane had
been parked earlier was a gigantic hole, several feet deep and several feet wide. There
was a pile of debris in one corner, resembling
what a small car might look like after being
hit by a speeding freight train. There wasn't
enough of the plane left to fill up the back
of a pickup truck.

One of the crewchiefs I talked to in the
area told me it used to be an A-37 Dragonfly
with a full load of fuel, bombs and ammo, all
set for a morning mission. Apparently, a
small piece of hot metal from the exploding
projectile hit the loaded plane, causing it to
disintegrate in one huge explosion. Luckily,
the explosion was contained by the steel and
cement revetment so no other planes were damaged by this one when it blew up.

I took a picture of that scene and moved
on. My friend and I saw an odd sight a little
ways down the row of revetments. It was
another A-37 which had been placed on three
saw horses. It had been severely damaged,
with no landing gear left to rest on, so it
had been placed up on the wooden stands. It
was pretty much a total loss too, but at
least it still looked like an airplane, unlike
the previous one.

We left this area and walked in between the
flightline and the revetments and came across a

small hole in the ground. What made this
hole unusual was the small piece of rocket
still in it. Explosive Ordinance Disposal
(EOD) personnel were about to rope off the
area so we only got a quick look at it. The
rocket had exploded, but the front end of it
had not completely blown up and was very vis-
ible. One of the EOD guys said that every
once in a while they'd come across a rocket
that had a timed explosive device in the nose
that was set to go off some time after the
initial hit. If anyone tried to pull it out
of the ground without disarming it first,
they'd get blown to bits. This particular
rocket had hit in some soft sand and would be
easy for them to get to. I was glad not to
have their job. There was enough danger just
being here near it. I took a picture of it
and left.

It was late morning now and we were getting very thirsty by this time. The heat and
humidity was getting to us during our long
walk around the base. We decided to walk
back to the terminal snack bar and get something to drink.

As we approached the damaged passenger
terminal from the flightline side, I noticed
that the windows had been blown out of the
second story of the Base Operations building.
One of the mortars that struck the flightline
had peppered the building with shrapnel. The
ground floor was protected by large cement
slabs, standing end-to-end, forming a protective barrier. Some of them weren't there
when I'd arrived last October. I'm sure they
must have saved some lives because there were
lots of different offices in that two story
wooden building. I used to deliver messages
to one of the offices around midnight every
night in my old job. I think the enemy knew
of the importance of the message center in
that building.

After a short break at the snack bar, we

decided to see what was left of the Airmen's
Club. Thin wisps of smoke drifted up from the
ruins when we arrived. It had been a fairly
large building and was now a small pile of
rubble on the cement foundation. There was a
rumor going around that some small arms ammo
was stored in one of its storage rooms, causing the secondary explosions and raging fire
that totally destroyed the structure. Some
people speculated that the club had been hit
by more than one rocket or mortar. In any
case, it seemed strange to us that this
building would burn down when so many others
had been hit in the attack and didn't burn at
all. Maybe it was all that alcohol! My barracks was only a couple of blocks away and I
thought how lucky I was, that it was this
building that was destroyed and not mine. It
certainly could have been. As a result of
the Airmen's Club being destroyed, everyone
under the rank of Sergeant was now allowed to
join the NCO Club. It was soon renamed the
Consolidated Open Mess since all enlisted
ranks were allowed to be members.

After taking a few pictures of the remains
of the Airmen's Club, my friend and I began
walking back to our barracks. Along the way,
we came across two barracks next to eachother
that had been damaged by the same explosion.

Several people were standing around, looking at the damage. We decided to have a look
too. A hot water heater that used to be con-
nected to the outside of one of the buildings
was now lying on the ground near a large
puddle of water. The water had drained from
the damaged water heater into the big hole
created by either an exploding rocket or mortar, nobody was sure which. I could clearly
see a second story room that had its outside
wall blasted open. There was some blood on
the white sheet that was on the bed next to
the wall that was damaged. The person who
was asleep there when the attack took place

had been wounded in the leg. The barracks
next to this one was not as badly damaged.
They both had large cement slabs lined along
the first floor walls and I'm sure that helped to minimize the damage and probably saved
some lives as well. The people who lived in
these barracks worked in the post office.
Their barracks looked identical to ours too.
Once again, I thanked God that it wasn't ours
that had been hit.

We got back to our barracks just before
noon and we talked about what we'd seen. I'd
used up a whole roll of film taking pictures
of everything I could find that had been damaged in the attack. I could hardly wait to
see the pictures after they were developed.
I only wished I'd had some color film instead
of black and white but since my paycheck
wasn't very big, I had to watch my expenses
carefully. Black and white film was a lot
cheaper to get developed than color film in
those days.

This attack had killed two Americans and
wounded fifteen. Vietnamese forces had none
killed with seventeen wounded. In Bien Hoa
City, twenty civilians had been killed. This
had been the most destructive attack on Bien
Hoa Air Base since I'd arrived. More planes
and buildings had been damaged and destroyed
than in previous attacks. It had made me
more nervous than any previous attack too.
This was the first time that I had actually
prayed to God during an attack. That's a
pretty good indication of just how bad it had
been. It only took a few minutes to pick up
the books and bug spray cans that had been
knocked off my wall shelves onto the floor.
It took a much longer time for the nightmares
to stop.

I found out later that day that the Vietnamese napalm storage area was hit and destroyed in the attack. Five rounds had hit
the 1st Cav area across the flightline from

us too. I just couldn't understand why the
North Vietnamese wanted to attack Bien Hoa
City and kill a bunch of innocent civilians.

On the radio news broadcast that night,
they said no base had ever been hit so much in
one attack with so many injuries. They also
said it was a North Vietnamese unit that did
it and that helicopters shot some of them
after it got light out when the unit was trying to leave the area.

I wrote a letter home that night telling
my family all about my exiciting first days
back at Bien Hoa. I didn't get to bed until
11p.m.and I had to be up at 5:30 a.m. It had
been a day I'll never forget for the rest of
my life.

I had to return to Tan Son Nhut Air Base
again on August 4th because I wasn't receiving any mail. For some unknown reason, my
mail was still being sent there even though
I'd filled out a change of address card before I left there on July 31st. Sending
someone's mail to the wrong base was not even
close to the most unusual thing that happened
lately.

A couple of my friends at Bien Hoa, both of
whom had been TDY with me to Tan Son Nhut, had
been declared AWOL (Absent Without Official
Leave) in Texas even though they were both
working here. Both of them got an assignment
to a base in Texas back in April but they were
never given any orders to go there and never
received a port call notification or anything
else that normally happens when you get a new
assignment. We found it really funny how
screwed up things could get. And that was just
the tip of the iceberg! So far, some of us
hadn't gotten paid regularly, some of us didn't
get our mail sent to the right base, didn't get
an assignment when we were told we would, and
now some were declared AWOL by the Air Force

because they had an assignment they weren't
even aware of!

The workload was so light now that I only
had to work from 6a.m. - 2p.m. What was so
strange in the schedule was that, after our
two days off, we were subject to stand-by
from 2a.m. -6a.m. even though we were scheduled to work from 6a.m. - 6p.m. They were
teaching me more about air freight paperwork
and how to properly load and unload aircraft,
how to put cargo pallets on a K-Loader, how
to put the cargo on the pallets and attach
the side and top nets and straps and things
like that. Basically, they were teaching me
the opposite of what I'd been taught at Tan
Son Nhut when I was taking things off instead
of putting things on.

I already knew how to drive a 10K forklift
but now I was learning how to drive a smaller
one, the 4K model. One of my co-workers was
so absent-minded one day that he accidentally
filled up his 4K forklift's radiator with gas
instead of water. He thought the radiator
cap was the gas cap. A lack of sleep will do
that to you sometimes.

I went to the 9a.m.Catholic mass the first
Sunday in August after the big attack. A
special prayer was said for one of the Marines that died in the attack. I also found
out that one of the seriously wounded also
died. There were holes in the walls of the
chapel to the right of the cross to remind us
of how close we were to God, one way or
another. There were more people in church
now than there used to be because of the
Marine unit that was now here from Japan. I
think the recent attack had something to do
with the increase in attendance too.

The Marines in my barracks must have complained up their chain of command about having no safe place to take shelter during an

attack. By August 5th they were tearing down
the old condemned shelters of wood and sandbags. They were replacing them with curved
steel shells covered with sandbags. Then they
put a second piece of curved steel over that
and topped it all off with another layer of
sandbags.

The Marines even brought their own cooks
and source of food supplies to the chow hall.
Now the food was really good, better than any
Air Force or Army chow hall I'd eaten in before. We could have steak and eggs for
breakfast just like the Marines. We never had
that before when the Air Force alone ran the
chow hall.

By August 10, 1972 I was really getting fed
up with the poor postal service in Vietnam.
I'd been at Bien Hoa for ten days by then and
I still wasn't getting any mail. I had to
travel back to Tan Son Nhut and try to find
out why. The people at the post office there
continued to put my mail in the General Delivery box, disregarding the change of address
card I'd filled out there back on July 31st.
I complained about it again, hoping they would
stop keeping it and forward it like they were
supposed to do.

As if that didn't make me mad enough, my
check for the July portion of my TDY was lost
somewhere and nobody at the Bien Hoa finance
office nor the one at Tan Son Nhut knew where
it was. The eight of us who went TDY together
all filled out travel vouchers and gave them
copies of our orders and we were told that our
checks would arrive in a week. The Tan Son
Nhut post office had some of my mail, but not
my check.

To add insult to injury, after getting back
to Bien Hoa around 4 p.m. after an all-day
attempt to get my mail and pay screw-up
straightened out, I got the news that seven of
us were going back to Tan Son Nhut to work any

day now and I'd have to start packing again.
By the time I got back to Tan Son Nhut, my
mail would all be forwarded to Bien Hoa!

Some guys who were TDY with me at Tan Son
Nhut didn't even get their regular pay
checks in addition to not receiving their
TDY pay. That's where I got lucky. My regular paycheck was the only one out of eight
people that was found at Bien Hoa. Shortly
after that, three other guys got paid. The
rest had to wait a while longer.

Another thing I found out while I was gone
to Tan Son Nhut was that a large NVA (North
Vietnamese Army) unit attacked a refugee camp
only 5 kilometers from Bien Hoa at 10:30 a.m.
They killed over 400 civilians and a South
Vietnamese military unit near there suffered
60% casualties. Then the NVA hit a small
U.S. Army camp, located just on the other
side of the 1st Cav area not far from here
with five 122mm rockets, followed by a
ground attack.

The American unit was "standing down,"
getting ready to return to the States. All
of their guns, ammunition, personal belongings, etc. were packed away except for a few
M-60 machine guns around the camp perimeter.

Some of the guys I talked to who helped
beat back the attack, said some of the
attackers wore uniforms while others wore
black pajamas. They said that some trucks
drove out of the woods and unloaded between
150 to 200 NVA who got through all but one
row of barbed wire before planes from Bien
Hoa Air Base started attacking them. They
said one GI in a guard tower held them off
for awhile by himself even after he was
wounded by an RPG (rocket-propelled grenade)
called a B-40.

By the time everyone got their rifles and
ammo out of the crates, the NVA were all over
the perimeter. Some of the GIs only had a

few clips of ammo and the planes came just in time. They said that spotter planes marked certain areas in the woods where tanks were spotted and several were destroyed. They estimated that around 15 tanks and 2,000 NVA were in an area less than 5 miles from Bien Hoa, probably the ones who shelled us last week with all those rockets and mortars.

It was good to get to talk to people who were actually involved in the battle instead of getting second-hand news from the TV, radio or newspaper. Sometimes their news stories weren't always accurate and didn't tell the whole story. In this case, I was able to find out what really happened and just how dangerous things were getting around Bien Hoa. I never would have imagined that enemy tanks would get that close to this base. That was more proof that the Communist Easter Offensive wasn't over yet.

Around the 17th or 18th of August I went to Tan Son Nhut Air Base again about my mail and TDY pay problems. I also went to visit Lin. I found out during that visit that she'd had a miscarriage on August 11th. A friend of hers took her to a hospital. When I got to her house in Cholon, she was still crying about it. She told me that she had stubbed her toe, the one that was hurt bad in a motorcycle accident, on the wooden stairs in her house and fell onto her side.

While I was visiting with her, she had to have some glucose given to her intraveinously. It took $3\frac{1}{2}$ hours from start to finish. I was there through the entire time. She said that she was in her 3rd month of pregnancy, according to her doctor. She was able to eat food now but was still not very strong after loosing the baby. I don't remember if it was a girl or boy. I may have asked her but I just can't remember. I felt so bad, so helpless.

After a couple of trips between Bien Hoa

and Tan Son Nhut trying to get my mail and
pay problems solved, having to complain to
the First Sergeant, Commander, the people in
charge of both base finance offices and post
offices, and now this. I was drained emo-
tionally and physically. I ended up making
a 3rd trip to Finance at Tan Son Nhut because they wanted me to sign some kind of
statement about not getting paid before they
would give me a new check. I think the only
reason they did that was because I threaten-
ed to go to the I.G. (Inspector General) and
my Congressman.

Upon returning to Bien Hoa, I had to go
back to Finance again because one of my
friends told me that the finance officer told
him that I'd been overpaid and owed the
government about $80.00. When I saw the
officer the next day, I told him they'd have
to take the money out of my next paycheck because I'd just spent my TDY money on doctor
bills in Saigon and since the mistake was
theirs, they'd have to correct it because I
didn't have the money to repay them.

Because of my crazy work schedule and all
those problems I was having at the time, I
didn't write to my family as much as I used
to. There just wasn't time. August was not
a good month for me, or for Lin either for
that matter. She'd been getting penecillin
shots and multiple vitamin pills to help
make her stronger. By August 28th, she looked like she was back to normal again. All of
the baby clothes and maternity clothes that
my parents had sent were given to some of her
relatives.

Lin and I had to attend a pre-marital
counseling session at the Tan Son Nhut Air
Base chapel on August 28th. The attendees
all got a nice certificate suitable for fram-
ing. The course covered all aspects of marriage. There were a dozen couples in our

class.

I thought that by sometime in September we'd be able to get married. We had not decided for sure if I would go to Clark Air Base by myself first and find us a place to live and then send for her or go together even if I had to stay in Vietnam longer in case the paperwork still wasn't done yet. I still did not have orders for Clark Air Base either. I was still sure I'd go there, based on the guy at CBPO telling me he'd seen the assignment papers.

The Viet Cong claimed on the radio that their attack on Bien Hoa August 1st had killed one U.S. general, 21 other Americans and 450 Vietnamese. They really made some ridiculous claims.

I was in Saigon on my day off visiting Lin on August 31, 1972. It's a good thing too because at 6:10 a.m. between 20 to 30 rockets slammed into Bien Hoa Air Base. The guys I worked with were at the hot cargo ramp unloading a C-141 Starlifter, a four-engined jet cargo plane capable of carrying ten pallets of cargo.

The hot cargo ramp is where they parked aircraft that had explosive cargo on them like artillery shells, bombs, rockets, tank ammunition, small arms ammo, etc. It was an extremely dangerous place to be during a rocket attack.

My friends were all in or directly behind the plane on a K-loader, a large yellow flat-topped machine with steel rollers on it so cargo pallets could be loaded onto or off of aircraft easily.

When the rocket explosions began, they all jumped down to the cement ramp and then split up trying to find a safe place to take cover. Some of them ran to a nearby cement drainage ditch. Those who did, got scratched up from the gravel along the edge of the ramp and the

rough surface of the ditch itself. One of
my friends in that group banged his knee so
hard, he ended up with a condition known as
water on the knee and had to have it drained
later on in the dispensary. He was on
crutches for awhile. He received a purple
heart medal for his injury incurred in the
attack.

A couple of the guys crawled under the K-
loader and one of them ran to a small building about 75 yards away. Some of the guys
jumped into a ditch that was full of mud and
water right next to the runway.

The plane they all had been on received
some shrapnel holes in the tail. The runway
and ramp behind the plane was cratered by
the exploding rockets. A C-7 Caribou cargo
plane that was parked near where I worked
had its ramp door blown off, its gas tanks
ruptured and had many shrapnel holes in it.
One A-37 Dragonfly fighter-bomber took a direct hit and the plane and its two 500 pound
bombs blew up in a huge explosion.

The enemy only targeted the runway area
of the base this time but still ended up
killing one American and wounding 31 others.
There were no Vietnamese casualties this
time. If the C-141 my friends were on had
taken a direct hit, at least 12 more Americans would have died.

When I got back from Saigon, they told me
how lucky I was. Out of eleven attacks that
year, I was in Saigon during three of them.
One of my friends jokingly told me to let
him know when I was going to Saigon again so
he could go too. Just call me lucky.

The reason I had gone to Saigon was not
just to visit Lin. I had to go to the CBPO
at Tan Son Nhut and check on the progress of
my marriage paperwork. The sergeant I spoke
to there said the results would be back any
day now. He explained that a private agency
hired by the U.S. government checks on the

paperwork to make sure someone isn't a security risk or a questionable character and then
someone at MACV Headquarters signs a paper
saying I can get married and then arrangements
are made at the American embassy. I felt like
I was running out of time.

I just missed the bus at MACV Headquarters
that would have taken me back to Bien Hoa. I
was in a panic because in a few hours I had to
be at work. I saw a Vietnamese guy who noticed me looking around as if I was looking for
a taxi, which I was. He said that he could
drive me to Long Binh Army Base for a set fee.
He had an old black car that looked like something the German Army drove in those old
World War II movies. I got in the back and
hoped he wasn't a Viet Cong on a mission to
snatch an American GI. I always had a suspicious mind. We made the trip to Long Binh
with no problems.

I spoke with the gate guards there and explained to them that I had missed the regular
shuttle bus that ran between MACV Headquarters
and USARV Headquarters at Long Binh and Bien
Hoa Air Base. I asked them if I could stay
near their gate and try and find a ride back
to Bien Hoa. I was wearing my khaki uniform
that day and they said I could as they were
willing to help a fellow GI out.

I asked the driver of a deuce-and-a-half
that pulled up to the gate if he was going to
Bien Hoa. He said yes and told me to climb
in the back. There was no room in the cab
because the guy next to him was holding a 12-
guage pump shotgun. They were both Marines
and their unit was at Bien Hoa now. I felt
lucky to have found a ride the rest of the way
without having waited very long.

I climbed in the back and sat on one of the
side-facing wooden fold-down bench seats.
There was already someone sitting in the back.
Another Air Force guy in khakis was returning
to his unit at Bien Hoa too. He'd just gotten

released from the hospital after recovering
from having his appendix removed. He'd been
in the 3rd Field Hospital in Saigon, not far
from where I'd lived.

The ride was a little bumpy at times but
uneventful as we traveled from Long Binh Army
Base to Bien Hoa Air Base. As we neared Bien
Hoa City, headed towards a base gate I'd
never been through before, the deuce-and-a-
half stopped briefly.

The Marine who'd been "riding shotgun"
literally, got out of the cab. He then stood
up on the running board and held onto the
truck with his left hand and held the pump
12-guage shotgun on his right hip with his
right hand. I asked him what was going on
and he said that some VC in Bien Hoa City had
thrown grenades at passing military vehicles.
He had orders to shoot at anyone who suddenly
appeared in any window of a passing building
that might be trying to do that to us. He
then told both of us in the back to keep our
eyes open and yell out if we saw anyone about
to shoot at us or throw a grenade.

The Marine on the running board stuck his
head in the cab and told the driver to go.
We went the rest of the way to Bien Hoa Air
Base without stopping again. Best of all,
nobody threw a grenade or shot at us.

The first week in September and FIGMO! That was GI slang for "Finally, I Got My Orders!" Now it was official. I'd been assigned to the 604th MASS (Military Airlift Support Squadron), which was not in PACAF (Pacific Air Force) like my current unit was. They were a part of another major command, MAC (Military Airlift Command). APO San Francisco 96274 is what my orders read and I had to ask someone in CBPO what that was. I was told simply, Clark Air Base, Philippines.

My tentative estimated departure date from Bien Hoa was October 15, 1972. It was an un-accompanied tour with no travel time per-mitted. What that meant was that I'd be traveling alone and I'd get on a plane in Vietnam and a couple of hours later I'd get off in the Philippines with no in-between stops.

I'd talked to several guys who'd been sta-tioned there before and they said it was a dangerous place. One guy even told me to take my helmet and flak jacket if I could because it was so dangerous. There was a lot of anti-American sentiments there and the government was very unstable, having problems with armed groups who wanted to overthrow their own gov-ernment and lots of shootings and thefts and lawlessness in general. Oh great, I'm going from the frying pan into the fire, as they say.

As if I didn't have enough problems, if I was able to get married in Vietnam before leaving for the Philippines, I'd be hard-pressed for time to try and get my orders changed so I could take my wife on an accom-panied tour instead of leaving her behind and then having to get a passport for myself and a Vietnamese visa so I could return to Vietnam

again and try to get her out of there that
way.

One morning when I was in the Air Freight
office during shift-change, the doors and
windows in the building started rattling and
vibrating a lot. Everybody in the office
noticed it as soon as I did. I thought it
was an earthquake and said so out loud. I
looked around at the other guys to see their
reactions. Some of the guys agreed with me
but one guy disagreed. He went outside for
a minute and then came back inside, telling
us to come outside and see what he'd seen,
while pointing at a spot up in the clear
blue sky. We could see the contrails of
three B-52 bombers, far off in the distance.
Even though we couldn't see the planes, we'd
all heard about Arc Light missions that were
composed of three of these huge planes.

It was those planes dropping bombs that
caused the earthquake-like shaking of the
building. We figured they must have hit a
target from around 10 miles away from us. A
newspaper article said that B-52s had dropped
bombs as close as 21 miles from Saigon and
even closer than that to us.

U.S. Marine Corps A-4 Skyhawks from right
here at Bien Hoa had dropped bombs within 8
miles of us, trying to hit Communist bunkers
and also some others that were 16 miles
north of Saigon, which was also in the same
newspaper article. Enemy troop concentra-
tions brought in during the Easter Offensive
were still being fought near us. They had
taken over several hamlets only 15 to 18
miles north of Saigon. The war may have been
over as far as U.S. combat ground forces were
concerned but it was far from over for U.S.
military aircraft and those of us who were
still here.

Enemy attacks weren't the only things making news here the first week of September.

We had some terrible thunderstorms, some lasting up to 7 or 8 hours. A bolt of lightning
set off a Claymore mine by the runway near
where I worked and in the area that I'd helped
put in more barbed wire. At first, some
people thought that a rocket had exploded. It
was loud enough to make people in the Consolidated Open Mess (formerly the NCO Club) jump
under their tables for cover. In a combat
zone, duck and cover is rule number one. The
freight yard got flooded and so did my new
room in the barracks. My floor got all wet
and fortunately the only things I owned that
got wet were my shoes and boots. The lightning was so bad, we all stayed inside at work
and played chess or cards to pass the time.
One of the C-141s scheduled to land here with
some cargo was cancelled for a day. The
weather had to be pretty bad before the Air
Force would cancel a cargo mission in Vietnam.

I went to Saigon on September 10th to visit
Lin and discovered that the Army quit running
the shuttle bus between Bien Hoa and Long Binh
Army Base. I had to hitch-hike from one base
to another on military vehicles but I got to
Saigon just as quick.
She told me two things which were very sur-
prising to me. First, that she didn't want to
leave Vietnam until after Tet 1973 because of
a Buddhist superstition her father told her
about. He told her that to leave at the end
of the year would be bad luck and if she
stayed in her homeland until after their new
year celebration of Tet, she would have very
good luck.
Secondly, she didn't want me to call her
Lin anymore. She wanted to be called by her
Vietnamese name. The reason she gave me was
that a former American boyfriend gave her the
nickname of Lin four years ago but now that
she was going to marry me, she wanted to drop
the name that wasn't really hers anyway. She

said that as far as she knew, her Vietnamese name was the equivalent to Susan in English. To protect her identity and simplify things, the name Lin will continue to be used in this book.

A big change at work happened that week as well. We finally got some VNAF (Vietnamese Air Force) personnel in our section so we could train them to do our jobs. We were told that they would be taking over completely by the end of the month. They didn't speak much English and we didn't speak much Vietnamese, so we didn't think they could take over that fast.

One of the VNAF I was training played a guitar on his lunch break. I asked him if he could teach me and he said yes. I had been taught some fundamentals of guitar playing by an uncle of mine in Georgia, but only the basics. I went to the souvineer shop where I'd bought my boonie hat and bought a guitar for only $5.00 in Piasters. By the time I left Vietnam, I could only play one song called House of the Rising Sun or something like that. As my way of repaying the guy, I gave him my guitar right before I left. Even though it was a cheap one, he really thought it was a great gift.

Guess what else happened while I was in Saigon on September 10, 1972? If you said that Bien Hoa Air Base got attacked again, you're right! My friends couldn't believe it happened a fourth time and one of them even joked that maybe my Vietnamese girlfriend was working for the VC and told her friends only to attack the base when I wasn't there.

At 10 a.m. that Sunday, September 10th, eleven rockets struck Bien Hoa Air Base. One of the one hundred pound 122mm rockets hit a pile of 200 stored bombs that all blew up in a tremendous explosion. Four M-48 tanks belonging to the South Vietnamese Army were destroyed. Two of their soldiers were killed

and ten were wounded. Across the base, 29
Americans were wounded and none were killed.
The concussion from that one blast caused by
all those bombs going off at once was so
powerful, the huge sliding doors on our
freight warehouse were knocked out of their
tracks and were stuck for awhile.

    Earlier that year I had written home
about how I felt when I was on guard duty one
night as a security police augmentee. They
gave me a hand-held radio, no weapon of any
kind, and was given an area of the base to
patrol. I told my parents that my instructions were to call in any sightings of the
enemy and hide.
When you're walking your "beat" down a
road on base with buildings on both sides of
the road or chain-link fences that border
supply areas, where can you hide? The street
lights made you an easy target for the enemy.
My mother got upset about the situation I
described to her, especially after hearing
stories about the Korean War from Daddy. In
that war, GIs that were on guard duty were
always armed. She wrote to President Nixon
to complain about her son in a war zone having to be on guard duty without a weapon to
protect himself with.
Presidents rarely reply personally to the
mail they recieve. Her reply came from the
Department of the Air Force. She later sent
the reply letter to me so I could read it and
know that the upper part of my chain of comm-
and didn't have any common sense and didn't
know how to deal with reality.
Their ridiculous policies were in a sense
a gamble with my life. They were willing to
bet that I wouldn't get killed while unarmed
on guard duty. They obviously had not served
in Vietnam in any capacity where their lives
were in danger nor did they pay any attention
to the facts that the VC had, and still were,

sneaking onto this base and other bases at
night and blowing things up and killing
people. Their policy of not arming ALL personnel performing guard duty was endangering
the lives of all of us that were unarmed in a
war zone.

This was what they told my mother in
their reply from the Department of the Air
Force, the office of the secretary dated
September 12, 1972:

Dear Mrs. Crews:

On behalf of President Nixon, this is
in further reply to your letter of
August 25, 1972, regarding the defense of
our personnel in Vietnam.

It is general policy in Vietnam to
issue arms and ammunition only to security
policemen, aircrew members and other
special category personnel while they are
on duty. During non-duty hours, the
weapons for these personnel and sufficient
weapons and ammunition for all other base
personnel are secured at central locations
to permit rapid issue should the need
arise. The Air Force has found this
policy minimizes firearm accidents and the
loss of weapons/ammunition to hostile or
criminal elements. Additionally, it re-
duces the possibility of uncoordinated
reaction to attack which can be extremely
dangerous and interferes with the actions
of security and defense forces.

In the event of attack, allied forces
are in place to provide immediate defensive protection. Should the combat situation become precarious, assistance is
readily available and will be used. The
defense of United States personnel in
Vietnam is of critical importance and is
reviewed on a continuing basis at the
highest government levels. The responsible commanders are confident that allied
plans, forces, and intelligence are equal

to the task of assuring the safety of essential residual American personnel.

I appreciate your interest in this matter and hope this information will be helpful.

Sincerely,
H.J. Anderson
Colonel, USAF

That letter just reinforced my belief that those in the upper levels of my chain of command had lost touch with reality. They had no clue in regards to the real situation here in Vietnam with regards to how the VC operate.

We'd already had VC sneak onto the base by crawling under barbed wire and around trip flares and Claymore mines. They set off their explosives, destroyed their targets and got back off base the same way they got in. At Cam Ranh Bay, some VC attacked unarmed Air Force personnel in their barracks with explosive satchel charges, killing and wounding dozens of GIs.

Keeping weapons locked up in a central location might work in a war with front lines but not Vietnam. If the higher-ups were so worried about accidents and theft losses, they should have had a policy that provided for more weapons training and weapons security.

As far as giving weapons to "other special category personnel while they are on duty," that should have included people like me who were standing guard duty, sometimes directly augmenting security police forces and protecting our base, ourselves, and base assets, all while on duty. Oh, but we can't be trusted according to "policy." You see what I had to deal with? My leaders in Washington made surviving my tour at Bien Hoa that much harder for me. I just got lucky, that's all.

And speaking about luck, the rocket attack on September 10th did more damage than I had initially been told. I found out on the 12th

that 75 helicopters on the Vietnamese side
of the base had been damaged. Windows all
over the base were broken, stuff got knocked
off the shelves in our barracks and pieces
of shrapnel up to 75 pounds hit our barracks
which was almost a mile from the blast site
where all those bombs went off at once. My
friends said the concussion hurt their ears
and really shook them up, even making the
ground shake like an earthquake.

On September 13th, I talked to a sergeant
on the phone who worked at the CBPO at Tan
Son Nhut Air Base where I had turned in my
marriage paperwork months ago. He told me
that my paperwork was back from the OSI
(Office of Special Investigations). He said
that it all checked out OK and today he was
going to take it to MACV Headquarters for
the final signature. He told me to call him
on Friday September 15th to see if it had
been signed. After that, I would have to
take all the paperwork to the American embassy and then I could get married.
I also got my port call on the 13th. I'd
be leaving Vietnam on October 23, 1972. I
had to leave out of Tan Son Nhut since we
had no commercial passenger flights leaving
from Bien Hoa any more. My Continental Airlines Boeing 707 was scheduled to leave at
1225 p.m. Some of my friends from tech
school were scheduled to leave on the same
flight. I'd be the only one of this small
group to get off at Clark Air Base, Philippines. The rest of them had gotten stateside assignments and would continue on, until the plane reached Travis Air Force Base,
California.

On September 14th I visited Lin and told
her when I'd be leaving. We were running
out of time if we were to get married before
I left. We talked for six and a half hours
about what we were going to do. There were

still many unanswered questions, so we could
not make any plans that were for certain, not
even our wedding day. I knew the Air Force
would release me from duty and send me to Tan
Son Nhut a couple of days before my plane
left. I was hoping that we could get married
by October 20th in the American embassy chapel
in Saigon if there wasn't enough time to get
married at the Bien Hoa chapel as we originally planned.

It was raining hard during this trip to
Saigon and I witnessed some bad accidents from
the inside of my taxi. Several motorcycles
got wiped out on one street by big trucks that
they rode too close to. My taxi even hit one
motorcycle but the rider wasn't hurt badly,
just wet, scratched up some, and very mad.

The taxi driver told me to get out and run
away before the police showed up because he
said the police in this part of town would demand that I pay the motorcycle rider a lot of
money and may ask for some for themselves. I
got soaked by the downpour as I left the area
and got into another taxi a few blocks away.

On September 15th I called CBPO at Tan Son
Nhut again to find out if my paperwork had
been signed. I couldn't reach the sergeant I
spoke to before and was told that nobody else
could help me and that I should call back on
Monday, September 18th. More time lost!

I was in line at the chow hall at Bien Hoa
that day when a sergeant that worked there
was telling everyone going through the line
that we were under a red alert starting that
night because MACV Headquarters had gotten
attacked. That made me wonder if that was why
I couldn't get hold of the sergeant at Tan Son
Nhut because he was going to MACV Headquarters
about my marriage paperwork.

I was headed for the snack bar near the
passenger terminal one day that week in September and I noticed some GIs guarding some

Vietnamese who were wearing black pajamas.
The two Vietnamese were squatting down in
the parking lot and the three GIs were
standing over them, talking to eachother. My
curiosity got the best of me and I walked
over to them to find out what was going on.
The Vietnamese had their hands tied behind
their backs and didn't make a sound.

One of the U.S. Army troops told me that
they had found these VC just walking around
in a daze a little over a mile from where
some bombs dropped from B-52s had exploded
and turned the earth into a scene like craters on the moon. The soldiers were working
with some South Vietnamese troops on a bomb
damage assessment mission north of Saigon, a
few miles west of here.

They said that huge trees were blown down
and were lying around on the ground like
those toy pick-up sticks. They found some
dead VC almost a mile from there that didn't
have a scratch on them. The concussion had
turned their insides to jelly. Blood was
running out of their ears, eyes, noses and
mouths. The few survivors they found were
further away from the crators and were too
stunned to offer any resistance. They were
now waiting for a ride back to their base
camp west of here.

That's how I found out about a lot of
things that happened here, by talking to
people. You couldn't depend on the newspaper or TV news to get the stories right
half the time.

On September 18th I went to Tan Son Nhut
to pick up my marriage paperwork. Then I
took a taxi over to the American embassy and
paid a fee of $2.50 to have three papers
notarized. I got to talk to the American
consulate, a very nice elderly lady. By the
time I got done at the embassy it was time
to head back to Bien Hoa. I had trouble

finding a ride from Saigon in a military
vehicle, so I hired a guy with a motorcycle to
take me to Long Binh Army Base. I'd never
seen an American in uniform riding on the back
of a motorcycle driven by a Vietnamese civilian and I was probably one of only a few that
were willing to try it. I made a big target
for any VC in the area but I was not going to
be late getting back, no matter what.

On September 19th I found out that it would
be my last night on the night shift. Everybody on night shift was going to be put on the
day shift because our unit didn't have enough
people left to split us up into two shifts
any longer. The good news was that we'd be
working a 3-and-1 schedule, three days of work
followed by one day off. That sure beat the
9-and-1 schedule that I first started out on
last October.

I visited Lin in Cholon on Friday, September 22nd. We took the marriage paperwork to
the Vietnamese Marriage Registrar but we
couldn't get anything done there that day. I
don't remember the specific reason why but because I wrote home about it, I know that's
what happened.

The BX ran out of color film and black ink
pens, even blue ones too. For awhile I could
take only black and white photos and all my
letters home were written in red ink.

Around this time I found out that Ferdin-
and Marcos, President of the Philippines, had
declared martial law because things were so
bad in that country. Everyone I talked to
that had been stationed at Clark Air Base
said it wasn't safe to live off base there. I
couldn't get my name on the base housing list
without already being married so Lin and I decided that she would stay with her family in
Vietnam for awhile.

She planned on selling her two-room house
in Cholon. When she bought it several years
ago, she paid only $250.00 for it in Pias-
ters. Because of inflation, it would cost
$1,000.00 now so she could make a good profit
from the sale of it. A 50cc motorcycle cost
only $200.00 a few years ago in Saigon. Now
they sold for $650.00 in Piasters. The war
destroyed the economy here and when all the
Americans were gone and all the jobs they
provided for the Vietnamese were gone too,
it would get much worse.

I went back to Saigon around September
25th and Lin was so sick then that we could
not take our marriage paperwork anywhere to
finish the Vietnamese requirements to get
married. At least all of the American government requirements had been met, but there
were still a few more things to do. I never
found out what made her so sick and she
didn't know either. She got better in a
couple of days.

In the letters I got from home, my mother
kept asking me about wedding announcements
and told me it was customary for the bride's
parents to make the announcements. We could
not tell anyone anything yet because we did
not know ourselves when we were getting married. Not only that, Lin told me that she'd
never heard of such a custom. Neither her
father, mother nor step-mother could speak
any English so they weren't capable of doing
something like wedding announcements. Those
were unknown to them as well.

A Catholic missionary priest would perform
the sacrament of matrimony at the American
embassy for us if we got all of the paperwork
done before I left. Since there wasn't much
time left, we decided against having the
ceremony at Bien Hoa. Lin had agreed to become a Catholic. Her step-mother was Catholic but she and her parents were Buddhists.

On the last Friday in September, we went
to the Vietnamese Marriage Registrar's office
in Saigon. They told us that we needed some
more paperwork done before we could get married. I needed to get a paper that told where
I worked and she needed to get a paper that
had her family tree on it. It seemed like
every time I thought we'd done everything on
the list we were supposed to do, something
else that was not on the list was required.
It was getting hard not to get mad about this
never-ending list of things to do.

Back at Bien Hoa Air Base, about twenty
five of us attended our last Commander's Call
on September 30, 1972. There had been over
200 members of Detachment 5, 8th Aerial Port
Squadron when I arrived last October. We
were given a nice wooden wall plaque with a
map of South Vietnam on it and the crossed
flags of both countries and our names and
dates of our tours at the bottom. We also
received a nice ciggerette lighter with in-
scriptions on both sides. Mine had:

Side 1	Side 2
STEPHEN A. CREWS	ONE HAS NEVER
DET. 5, 8 AP SQ	LIVED TIL HE HAS
BIEN HOA AB	ALMOST DIED, LIFE
VIETNAM	HAS A FLAVOR THE
1972	PROTECTED WILL
	NEVER KNOW

That night I wrote home and asked my parents to go to the place in Newnan, Georgia
where you register to vote and get their address for me. I'd already sent in two Military Overseas voter registration cards and
never received an absentee ballot or anything
and I was 21 years old now and wanted to vote
in the upcoming presidential election.

I started my out-processing from my unit
on October 2, 1972. Back then, you went to
your unit orderly room and gave them some
copies of your PCS (Permanent Change of Station) orders. In return, they gave you a
paper with a long list of places to go and
you had to get someone's initials next to
each location listed. Some of the places on
the list were: CBPO, post office, education
office, dispensary, library, finance office,
etc.

My unit was going to release me from my
assignment there on October 21st. Until
then, I still had to turn in my gas mask,
helmet and flak jacket. I had a lot of
places to walk to around the base in the
heat, humidity and sometimes the rain. Lots
of walking. I'd be leaving Bien Hoa for Tan
Son Nhut on the afternoon of October 21st.
Short! 21 days and a wake up!

I found out that another guy in my unit
was having the same problems in getting
married as I was and he hired a lawyer to
get the passport and visa as well as marriage paperwork done, all in 20 days on a
C.O.D. (Collect On Delivery) basis. It
would cost him $350.00 if it was all done in
time. It would cost him nothing if it all
wasn't done in 20 days. I was very tempted
to do that too, but I held onto my money and
pressed on by myself because I was so close
to being finished.

One of the guys who left here a month ago
to get out of the Air Force, came back here
on a 90-day tourist visa as a civilian so he
could try and get his fiancee's paperwork
done. He'd been working on it for eight
months and it was supposed to take only two

months. He and I agreed that to us, it seemed
like the Vietnamese officials tried to hamper
the efforts of couples trying to get married,
any way they could.

I was working on day shift that first week
of October 1972. The shift hours were from
6 a.m.- 6 p.m. The beginning of October was
just like the end of September, rain, rain,
and more rain. Sometimes I had to board civilian aircraft carrying only cargo pallets and
help push heavy pallets onto the K-loaders, in
addition to my normal job of breaking down
pallets of cargo and checking each piece of
cargo against the manifest. Then I had to
place each piece in a designated area of the
freight yard just like I'd learned to do while
TDY to Tan Son Nhut Air Base. Just like before, FB5250 (Base Supply) got the majority of
the cargo we received.

The heat and humidity continued to torment
me and everyone else. It was impossible to
stay dry. Either you got soaked in your own
sweat or by the rain showers or both. I got
into the habit of keeping my wallet in a plastic bag so the contents would stay dry.

Around this time my parents sent me a couple of boxes of clothes. One of them had used
clothes that were going to be given to the
Salvation Army and the other one was for Lin
and I. On my next trip to Cholon, we gave the
box of used clothing to a family with kids
that lived near her. When Lin told them the
clothes came from the United States, they were
so happy and grateful. You'd have thought
Santa Claus himself had shown up at their door
by the looks on their faces. It made me feel
so good to see the happiness that simple gift
brought to that family. I told my parents in
my next letter that they made a big difference
in those poor people's lives with the clothes.

On October 3rd I gave Lin the paper that

was signed by my commander and listing Bien
Hoa Air Base as my residence and where I
worked. That may have been on the same trip
when I brought the two boxes of clothes with
me. She was going to take that paper, along
with her family tree paper back to the
office that asked for them in Saigon by herself. She thought that if I wasn't there
with her, the people there might be a little
bit more inclined to help get things done
quicker.

I don't know how many trips I'd made from
Bien Hoa to Saigon in 1972 but I know it was
a lot. Most of the time the trip took from
45 minutes to an hour. When I had to hitch-
hike, it sometimes took closer to $1\frac{1}{2}$ hours.

On this trip, I remember asking her what
that noise was that I heard in the middle of
the night through her thin plywood walls.
I'd heard sounds and low voices too. She
told me that there were some American GIs
who had deserted and lived with their Vietnamese girlfriends in one of the apartments
that adjoined her little house. She said
that they stayed hidden all the time and at
night is when they could be heard because it
was so quiet in this part of Cholon, Saigon
in the middle of the night.

I'd read some books in the past couple of
years that mentioned opium dens in different
cities in China and elsewhere in Asia and
they described how the black tar opium was
smoked. Different people smoked it for
different reasons. One night Lin decided to
smoke some in my presence for the first time
and I was shocked. I had no idea that she
had ever smoked opium because she'd never
mentioned it and I'd never seen any around
or seen her in a "mellow" state.

She told me that she had been smoking it
for years as part of her religious beliefs
and to help ease the pain of losing her brother in the battle of Quan Tri this year.

She had what looked like a tar ball wrapped up in a piece of plastic wrap. She lit an oil lamp on the floor and put the tar ball, which was the opium, on a metal rod that was about 6 inches long. She rotated the black tar opium on the rod over the flame of the lamp to soften it and then put it in a pipe and began smoking it. She was lying on a mat on the floor at this time.

She told me that she wouldn't allow me to try it even if I wanted to. After smoking the opium, she appeared to be relaxed and somewhat "mellow" like some people I'd seen at Bien Hoa after they'd smoked marijuana. We discussed her having to pass a drug test before leaving Vietnam and she told me that she knew of a drug de-tox center, kind of like a modern-day rehab center that exists in our country today that she would go to soon.

She was saddened by her brother's death and saddened at having a miscarriage and saddened that I might be leaving here without us getting married first. She turned to the opium as her way to get rid of the sadness. She wanted to spend this night with me, one which may be our last night together and not be in a sad mood.

As we hugged eachother before falling asleep, all I could say about the eye-opener with the opium was, it worked. I never tried it and hoped that she would be able to pass a drug test when the time came. The smell of the incense sticks she'd lit before she began smoking had covered up the smell of the opium, which had a very distinctive smell. It was a sure sign that she'd done this before. I could only hope that it would be the last.

I talked to a guy who was TDY from Clark Air Base on October 4th. We were so short of people now that the Air Force was sending others here on temporary duty. He gave me a lot of information about what it was like on

and off base and the news about conditions
off base was pretty bad. They had a curfew
at night and the local cops could shoot anyone outside after curfew.

The only good news was that rent was only
$50 to $60 a month for a small furnished one
bedroom apartment.

I made another trip to Saigon on October
8th to see Lin and to check on the progress
of our marriage paperwork. She didn't have
her family tree paper done because she had
to get some members of her family to help
her and they had not returned it to her yet.
With only two weeks left before I had to
leave for the Philippines, I was really
worried that we wouldn't get everything done
in time.

A new night shift was created again on
October 9th after not having one for several
weeks, and I got put on it. They told everyone that there would be no more days off until we got relieved from duty just prior to
leaving the country. At this time I was
told I'd be relieved on October 18th and so
I'd have to work eight straight days from 7
p.m.-7 a.m. We used to work from 6 to 6 but
that changed now.

The reason a lot of us were put on a new
night shift was because the NCOs wanted to
stay on day shift and do all of the training of the Vietnamese military and a few
American civilians during daylight hours.

During the beginning of the second week
of October, I packed and re-packed my duffle
bag so I wouldn't go over the 66-pound
weight limit they gave us on baggage. I
ended up having to mail some stuff because
of that limit.

One of my friends got married in Saigon
the first week in October. I didn't find
out for awhile because he was working on a

different shift and was on leave. Another one of my friends was getting married on October 15th. He'd paid a lawyer to get his paperwork done faster. In hindsight, maybe I should have done that too. It looked like I wasn't the only GI in my unit going home with a war bride, that is, if the paperwork ever got done in time.

I think the term "war bride" originated in World War II. Lots of American GIs got married to women from Australia, England, France and some other European countries. Since those marriages happened during or shortly after the war, "war bride" became a new term.

Just minutes before I got off work early in the morning on October 11th, I was in the Traffic Control office talking with some friends. Suddenly, the door to the office started rattling a lot and then rumbling sounds made the air seem to vibrate. Everyone in the office went outside and we saw lots of long white contrails in the sky, all headed in the same direction. Two flights of B-52 bombers, with three planes flying in a "V" formation in each flight, one flight behind the other, were flying low enough that we could see the individual planes. They were high enough to be safe from ground fire.

I thought they were bombing around Highway 13, about 7 to 10 miles west of Bien Hoa. It was quite an experience to actually see them about 30 seconds after the rumbling stopped. I'd hate to be anywhere near where the target was.

I had to go to Tan Son Nhut Air Base on October 12th to send my box of hold baggage. It weighed 80 pounds. I got the wooden seachest, or footlocker as I called it from some Navy Seabees that used to be stationed just down the road a short distance from Bien Hoa.

After leaving that base I went to see Lin

but could only visit her for an hour before
heading back to Bien Hoa. She still didn't
have the family tree paper yet and she was
taking this problem very hard.

Some B-52s bombed somewhere close by
again while I was working one night, the
13th of October I believe it was. As in the
previous bombing, the ground shook and it
felt like the same distance as before. I'd
been right in guessing where they were bombing on the 11th. The Stars and Stripes
newspaper on the 12th ran a big story about
it on the front page, "Reds in Hamlets Near
Saigon."

North Vietnamese troops had taken over a
bunch of places north of Saigon and west of
here and Highway 13 was cut 20 miles north
of Saigon for the fourth consecutive day.
There were so many North Vietnamese troops
within striking distance of Bien Hoa that
the Marines guarding pórtions of the base
perimeter at Bien Hoa and key sections of
the runways, were put on a standby alert.
They were told to expect rockets and possibly a ground attack.

As I was writing a letter to my parents
on October 14th, my room in the barracks
started shaking and I could hear the BOOM,
BOOM, BOOM of the bombs exploding from the
B-52s. It was incredible to feel the ground
shake miles away from the target area.

Sometime between October 15th and 18th, I
made another trip to Saigon. This time, Lin
had the family tree paper and we went back
to the Vietnamese Marriage Registrar's
Office. After turning in the final documents
they wanted from us, the guy in charge explained what would happen next. He prepared
a document that was basically an announcement
to the public of our intentions to get married. It was then posted on a bulletin board

where everyone could see it. It was called
"posting the bans of marriage." He told us
that it had to stay posted for ten days.
After ten days, if nobody came forward with a
reason why we shouldn't be allowed to be married, then the document would be taken down.

Then, he'd give us another paper which was
the Vietnamese government's permission to get
married. We could then take that paper to the
American embassy to show them and then we
could get married. I didn't understand a word
the guy said because he spoke so fast and my
Vietnamese vocabulary was very limited. It
was a good thing Lin could listen to him and
then translate it all into English for me. No
wonder my friend had hired a lawyer!

There was only one problem with what he
told us and it was a BIG problem. I would be
in the Philippines ten days from then. Lin
and I left that office feeling terrible.

After all those months of going to seminars
and briefings, filling out dozens of forms,
making many trips to Saigon and having physical exams and background checks done and now,
just when the paperwork was 99% done, the ten
day waiting period was a few days too many.

Around that time, a story was printed in
the Stars and Stripes newspaper that gave us
some hope. The story was about an Army veteran who married his Vietnamese girlfriend
after a two year separation. After he left
Vietnam at the end of his tour of duty and at
the end of his enlistment, he became a civilian. He returned to Vietnam and searched
refugee camps until he found some of his girlfriend's family members who helped him find
her.

The publicity surrounding his search for
her helped lead to a quick dispersal of the
red tape involved in getting married in Vietnam. He ended up getting her what is known as
a fiancee visa and they left Vietnam together
and got married in New York. As long as there

was a functioning South Vietnamese government, there was still hope for us yet.

Six of my friends and I got together one
night at the Consolidated Open Mess at Bien
Hoa for what some of us were calling "the
last supper." There was no longer a separate Airmen's or NCO or Officer's Club. Now
the three clubs were combined under one roof
and we all ate as equals now.
Everyone at our table were all graduates
of the same tech school. A couple of the
guys were from a different graduating class
than mine but that didn't matter. We had
all arrived at Bien Hoa Air Base the previous October, some on different planes and
on different days. Some of us had roomed
together and all of us had worked together,
if not in the same office, at least in the
same building. Some of us had even gone on
a TDY to Tan Son Nhut together. We had all
shared the same dangers too and I suppose
that made this last gathering at the supper
table a bit more special.
We'd all be leaving in a week or two and
knew that we might not ever see eachother
again. Though we came from different states
and different backgrounds, we all agreed that
we shared one particular thing in common. We
had all survived Bien Hoa, or "Ben Whoopee"
as some called it. We were some of the last
people to ever be a part of Detachment 5, 8th
Aerial Port Squadron and were proud of it.
We were a part of history now and felt like
eating together and sharing a bottle of wine
together so we could toast our good fortune.
As I recall, there was more than one toast
made that night. Everyone enjoyed the wine,
the food and our last get-together.

The day I left Bien Hoa Air Base for good
and went to Tan Son Nhut Air Base to check in
for my "freedom bird" to the Philippines, I

wasn't allowed to leave the billeting area.
I was both shocked and disappointed. I'd
planned on checking my duffle bag in, get my
boarding pass and then go see Lin one last
time before leaving.

The rule here was, once you checked in,
you couldn't leave the area. You had to stay
in the area until a bus came and took you to
your plane. Had I known that ahead of time,
I would have done things differently. Now I
had no way to say goodbye to Lin.

The next day, October 23, 1972, I sat in
my window seat on the plane bound for the
Philippines and looked out at the base one
last time. I don't remember actually crying
while I mentally told Lin goodbye, but I know
I felt like it. I felt frustrated and helpless, having to go along with things that
were out of my control.

After the plane was in the air and the
landing gear were up, some of my fellow military passengers broke into cheers and laughter. I was just as happy as they were to be
leaving the war in Vietnam behind me, happy
that I'd reached at least one particular goal
in life. In October 1971, surviving my tour
of duty at Bien Hoa was my number one goal
and now it was October 1972 and I'd made it
out in one piece.

My story ends with my physical departure
from Vietnam. Even though I'd left it, it
didn't leave me. Dreams, bad nightmares and
memories lingered on. I'm happy to say that
the dreams and bad nightmares stopped long
ago. The memories last a lifetime though, as
veterans of all wars can attest to.

As for Lin and I, my letters to her from
the Philippines went unanswered and I never
returned to Vietnam. Some things just weren't
meant to be, just like the war we could have
won but didn't.

14604552R00143

Made in the USA
Charleston, SC
20 September 2012